WITHDRAWN

BEING AND BECOMING

BEING AND BECOMING

AN ESSAY TOWARDS A CRITICAL METAPHYSIC

by

D. J. B. HAWKINS

SHEED AND WARD

NEW YORK · 1954

NIHIL OBSTAT: J. P. WROE, D.D., Ph.D.,
CENSOR DEPUTATUS.

IMPRIMATUR: ✠ CYRILLUS,
EPUS. SOUTHWARCEN.

SOUTHWARCI, DIE 24a JUNII 1954.

CONTENTS

FOREWORD

I AM well aware that I have not attained any final clearness on the topics treated in this book. But they are topics which offer an inexhaustible field for analysis, and my excuse for writing is that after reflecting on them for thirty years there may be enough that is new and enough understanding of what is old to make it worth while to present the results with a proper degree of humility. Moreover, attempts at a critical rethinking of the metaphysics of the Aristotelian and Thomistic tradition are not so common in the English language that even a highly imperfect instance of it should be regarded as superfluous.

Philosophers outside that tradition may well think that a great deal is taken for granted which seems to them to be highly problematic. That, after all, is the natural consequence of belonging to a tradition which gives satisfaction on the whole, whatever modifications and enlargements may seem desirable in detail. Yet it would be a pity if an essay such as this failed completely as communication to thinkers of other schools. The Aristotelian tradition can lay claim to precisely the qualities for which Lord Keynes, in the preface to his *Treatise on Probability*, praised the central succession of British philosophers, "who, in spite of their divergences of doctrine, are united in a preference for what is matter of fact, and have conceived their subject as a branch rather of science than of the creative imagination, prose writers, hoping to be understood". Going over the subject once again, I can only say that my admiration for Aristotle has been enhanced, and particularly my admiration for the way in which, so early in the history of philosophy, he was able to lay down a great part of a clear basic vocabulary for the

vii

expression of the most general and pervasive of notions. This aim is sufficiently close to the preoccupations of many contemporary British philosophers to solicit a hearing from them for a metaphysical essay in the Aristotelian tradition.

Some Thomists, on the other hand, may think that my personal suggestions are unwanted and ugly excrescences on an already complete and harmonious edifice. I can only say that these seem to me to be demanded by a rethinking of the ancient texts in conjunction with a due consideration of the contributions and criticisms of later philosophy. I hope, at least, that they will agree that such questions must be discussed in any living tradition of thought. It would be altogether misleading and regrettable if we gave the impression that Thomism was a kind of archaeological pursuit.

I have kept references and quotations to a minimum, using them only when they seemed really helpful in illustrating a problem or its history. A reader may be expected to give credit to a philosopher for having read the relevant material without having his time wasted by seeing it all rehashed in text and footnotes. If he has the laudable desire to read it all himself, the historians of philosophy are there to tell him where to find it. The approximately equal length of the chapters is due to their having originally been prepared as lectures, but, since the division seemed as good as any other, I have preserved it. For the benefit of those who are not already practised philosophers I have prefixed to the book an analysis of the contents. This will, I hope, enable the reader to find his way about without difficulty and will remind him both of what he has read and of what he is about to read.

The last three chapters cover the same ground as my book *Causality and Implication*, published in 1937 and now out of print. I do not think that what I said then was altogether wrong, but there are many things in that essay which now seem to me to amount to an intolerable logicization of reality, and I have tried to reformulate my opinions in such a way as to do justice to the difference between logic and metaphysics, between the order of thinking and the order of being.

D.J.B.H.

ANALYSIS OF CONTENTS

I. THE NEED OF A CRITICAL METAPHYSIC

1. General metaphysics or *ontology* was systematized rather late in the history of the Aristotelian tradition, and the results are in many respects unsatisfactory. Much work remains to be done in order to arrive at a metaphysic which both does justice to the sources and is adequate to the needs of today.

2. Hume made metaphysics impossible by both restricting his data to impressions and ideas and refusing to recognize necessary relationships which are not contained in the meaning of the terms. These, however, are arbitrary dogmas which need not inhibit our investigation.

3. Hume's philosophy becomes plausible only when we suppress as far as possible the *activity* of thinking. Kant saw that what was lacking in Hume had to be supplied by the activity of thinking, but assumed that what was thus supplied could only have a relative value in terms of human thinking about things as they appear, and could not apply to things in themselves. This is another arbitrary dogma which we are justified in disregarding, but Kant was right in singling out the importance of what he called the synthetic *a priori* judgment.

4. In our own day the logical positivists assign the task of eking out Hume to *linguistic construction* rather than to *a priori* thinking. A genuine philosophy of being must show that the activity of thought puts us into contact with real being and that there are primary evidences of *what is* which are the foundations of ontological thinking. Such evidences are not obvious in the sense of presenting themselves immediately to a superficial view, but are self-evident when discovered and understood as the result of conceptual analysis.

II. THE PROBLEMS OF BEING

1. *Being* has a variety of meanings, but its central and unambiguous application is to real existence. Moreover the real existent is individual. The main problems of being are those of *existence* and of *individuality*.

2. These problems remain in the background in ancient philosophy, because the possibility of non-existence, which is contingency and implies createdness, was not taken seriously, and because Platonism emphasized the species over the individual.

3. The problem of *existence* emerges in medieval philosophy with Avicenna, who regards existence as analogous to an accident of essence. The same tendency appears in Anselm, who talks in effect of an essence entailing its existence. But an essence cannot be properly regarded as prior to existence, for it is nothing apart from existence.

4. St. Thomas Aquinas revolutionizes the problem by enlarging existence into *being* as including all that is positive in the modes of being and thus reducing essence to a principle of *limitation*. But many later thinkers have continued to discuss the relation in Avicennian terms.

5. In the next generation Duns Scotus stresses the irreducible character of *individuality* or thisness but does not seem to have studied sufficiently the conditions of individuality or to have related it adequately to other factors of being.

III. THE ANALYSIS OF BEING

1. Logically we can speak of things as either existing or not existing. The subject of our thought is in this case an abstract description, and we must add, in order to satisfy the complete fact, that an existent thing is constituted as an individual. Even so, difficulties remain if we take this as a proper description of its ontological structure.

2. Bertrand Russell makes a determined but unsuccessful attempt to get rid of the embarrassing logical predicate of existence. Since Russell's solution is unacceptable, we must go back to Kant's discussion of existence as a predicate.

3. Kant makes clear that existence cannot be a real *predicate* or attribute, because there is nothing prior to it of which it could be an attribute. We may conclude that existence is more like an ultimate *subject*.

4. Existence is an *open* notion which cannot be dissociated from the forms that it takes. It is in antithesis only to the limitations which make a thing one of this sort or of that. Hence in the real order we find the basis of Aquinas's distinction, which, if we left essence and existence with their logical meanings, might be appropriately described as a real distinction between *being* and *quiddity*.

5. The objection that quiddity thus becomes a mere negation is answered by the fact that it is not only a principle of the limitation of being but a positive principle of individuality.

IV. DISTINCTION AND RELATEDNESS

1. Analytic thinking reveals distinctions and relationships within the realm of experience. Our business is not only to recognize them but to select those which best serve to exhibit the structure of the whole.

Hence there is a certain element of choice in the architecture of a metaphysical system.

2. Apart from purely verbal distinctions, *real distinctions* are those which subsist or appear when we are genuinely thinking in terms of being. There are also *logical distinctions* which involve no difference of real factors but have a foundation in fact in so far as being is such as to present these aspects in distinction to a thinking mind.

3. The modern logic of *relations* provides a useful vocabulary by which to classify them. Metaphysically, however, the main task is to distinguish between *real relations*, which subsist between really distinct factors, and *logical relations*, whose terms are only logically distinct. Originative relations are a source of new reality, for they are productive of one of their terms. But in no case does it appear that we are justified in asserting a relation to be really distinct from the term to which it is attributed.

V. SIMILARITY AND ANALOGY

1. The problem of *universals* must have ontological consequences, but the traditional classification of opinions under the heads of nominalism, conceptualism and realism does not seem on examination to be as clearcut as it sounds.

2. An historical survey shows that differences of opinion about the status of universals can be most usefully regarded as differences about the nature of *similarity*.

3. It is evident, on the one hand, that there are real similarities as well as similarities of name and, on the other, that a similarity is not a part which can be isolated from the parts which are dissimilar in two similar things. Even exact similarity is not reducible to partial identity. Similarity is in itself a primary and irreducible notion but is intelligible in relation to the two limiting notions of complete identity and absolute diversity.

4. The problem of *analogy* is an extension of that of similarity. Only the exactly similar is completely univocal; all other notions are in some degree analogous as being verified in different ways. Being is the completely and utterly analogous notion.

VI. UNITY, DIVERSITY AND NUMBER

1. Similarity and mutual exclusiveness are the conditions of numerability. *Numbers* are real relational properties of the groups to which they belong, but they are not really distinct from these groups.

2. Leibniz's principle of the *identity of indiscernibles* appears to be justified if we take into account not only intrinsic properties but originative relations with their spatial and temporal consequences.

3. Hence, while *individuality* is in itself an irreducible notion, it demands dissimilarity as a condition. Being is the principle of similarity, of analogy and of participation; quiddity is the principle of dissimilarity, of finite determination and of individuality.

4. Reflecting on the nature of metaphysical thinking, we see that it must use logic in order to transcend logic. We can begin only with our experience and thinking in its concreteness, but the aim of the metaphysician is to discern what is due simply to the way in which we come to know things and thus to penetrate to the structure of fact as it is in itself.

VII. Change, Potency and Act

1. The notion of *becoming* presupposes being. *Change* is a becoming in succession to a previous state of being. Change and changeability imply *time*, for time in its widest sense is the quantitative character of a successive continuum. *Continuous change* is conceivable but not observable.

2. The Aristotelian doctrine of *act* and *potency* is primarily an explanation of a changing thing. A thing cannot become simply anything else, but the range of its potentiality is limited. What it actually is at any moment is something within its permanent range of potentiality. Active powers and passive potentialities can be distinguished only roughly. The discrimination of potency and act is also made in a secondary and purely logical sense, in which they are equivalent to *determinable* and *determinant*. It is also applied to the relationship of essence and existence in yet another sense, for existence is *determinable but act* and essence is *determinant but potency*.

3. The *extrinsically possible* is that which is possible with reference to what is actually known to be; in this sense things are not only possible but more or less *probable*. *Intrinsic possibility* implies the absence of internal contradiction and therefore presupposes the notion of impossibility or internal contradiction. Only exhaustive knowledge of a thing, apart from awareness of its actual existence, can entitle us to assert positively that it is possible.

VIII. Substance

1. The doctrine of *substance* is an explanation of how a thing can change in certain respects while remaining fundamentally the same thing. Thus we are aware of a permanent self underlying its various activities and experiences.

2. The identity of a changing thing cannot reside in what it actually is at any moment but must consist in the unity of its potentialities and

powers. This is what Aristotle calls its *nature*. Substance is not a bare subject of predicates but the nature of the thing.

3. When substance is regarded merely as ultimate logical subject, it loses its ontological significance. Thus it was in Locke's conception. Descartes had previously tried to identify substance with a fundamental activity or attribute, but this is a complete misunderstanding. After Locke it was not unnatural that Berkeley should abolish the apparently useless notion of material substance and that Hume should go on to abolish mind. The concept of substance has not yet regained its proper meaning and importance in modern philosophy, although the *Existenz* of the existentialists goes some way towards its restoration.

4. *Substance* and its *attributes* are really distinct but they are one in the concrete. Substance, although only a unity of potentialities, can be said to be real because it is the positive individuality which possesses these potentialities.

5. The indication of a unity of substance is a distinctive *unity of behaviour*. Hence organisms are substances. Nevertheless the particles of which they are composed appear to continue to behave in many respects as they would behave outside an organism. The most natural explanation is that substance is an analogous term and that things can be one substance and many substances at the same time.

IX. VALUE

1. Value-judgments are not merely instances of the emotive use of language or statements of emotive attitudes.

2. It is not enough to say with Ewing that good is the fitting object of a pro-attitude or with Moore that it is undefinable.

3. *Good,* according to Aristotle, resides in the development and fulfilment of natural potentialities. This doctrine satisfies by fitting the facts.

4. Intrinsic *evil* is more than the absence of greater good, for it resides in the frustration of natural activity. That is still more fully evil which is the source of evil outside itself as well.

5. *Comparison* of values is sometimes but not always possible. In particular, we may doubt whether it is meaningful to ask what would be the best possible world.

X. CAUSALITY IN ARISTOTLE AND HUME

1. The Aristotelian division of *material, formal, efficient* and *final* causes applies most comfortably to human activity. In a more generalized form the causal problem concerns an originative relationship of antecedents to a consequent in accordance with a general law.

Analysis of Contents

2. Not only the statement that every effect has a cause but the statement that everything contingent has a cause seems on analysis to be tautologous. What is completely uncaused must be timeless and unchangeable. Hence whatever *begins to be* demands an adequate cause of being and usually has complete or partial temporal causal antecedents. The final ground of being caused resides in *finitude*.

3. Inductive logic vacillates between a reliance on *observed regularities*, which are inadequate to justify a genuine generalization, and an appeal to the *uniformity of nature*, which is difficult to formulate or to prove. The problem is to find an *initial probability* for the tentative generalizations which are tested and refined by scientific methods. A view of the world as composed of substances in simultaneous and successive interaction according to their natures supplies this probability and justifies the scientist's search for valid correlations.

4. The principle of *sufficient reason* does not seem to add anything to principles of causality in the *ontological* order, but in the *logical* order it signifies that every true proposition is either demonstrable or self-evident. This has the metaphysical consequence that all being is in principle *intelligible*. In the end it appears that being is destined to thought and that the primary mode of being is mental rather than material.

CHAPTER I

The Need of a Critical Metaphysic

I

OUTSIDE a fairly restricted philosophical circle the proposal to develop a general metaphysic or ontology comes nowadays with a somewhat antiquated air. The name itself has acquired a questionable reputation. Apart from the logical positivists, for whom a statement is metaphysical if, being incapable of verification, it is nevertheless gratuitously asserted, the majority of people regard as metaphysical what is alleged to pertain to a spiritual world beyond this world of space and time. The notion of a general metaphysic or ontology, which is the science of being and of those aspects of being in its generality which transcend the opposition of mind and matter, has fallen into oblivion. Yet it does not seem unreasonable to suppose that, starting from the world of experience, we should be able to refine our concepts sufficiently to construct such a science. The reasons for its contemporary neglect are reasons of history and not of principle.

In the first place, we must remember that metaphysics emerged rather late as a systematic discipline. The treatises lumped together under that name in the works of Aristotle on the ground that they came after the *Physics* are of very disparate character, and much of what we should now call Aristotle's metaphysics has to be sought in the *Physics* themselves. This applies, for example, to Aristotle's doctrine of causation. The medieval Aristotelians developed their metaphysical thinking as an adjunct to their theology and composed no systematic works on metaphysics. The systematization of metaphysics was a product of what we may call the silver age of Aristotelian scholasticism and is associated with the *Disputationes Metaphysicae* of Suarez. A hundred years later an equal and equally temporary impression was made by the *Ontologia* of Christian Wolff. The name of ontology seems to have been first suggested by Clauberg in his *Elementa Philosophiae sive Ontosophia* (1647). Ontology or ontosophy is there defined as "quaedam scientia quae contemplatur ens quatenus ens est, hoc est inquantum communem quamdam intelligitur habere naturam vel naturae gradum, qui rebus corporeis et incorporeis, Deo et creaturis, omnibusque adeo et singulis entibus suo modo inest".[1]

Now Suarez is far from being a negligible figure of scholastic decadence, nor is it Wolff's sole title to remembrance that he provided the kind of metaphysics that Kant criticized adversely, but neither Suarez nor Wolff is among the first rank of philosophers. In spite of the Thomist revival and the publication of innumerable manuals of would-be Thomistic metaphysics it must be confessed that the Suarezian and Wolffian modes of presentation have unconsciously influenced most of them, and their neat conceptual constructions tend to have an air of unreality. The most erudite of recent scholastic metaphysicians, Pedro Descoqs, the incomplete state of whose projected treatise is much to be regretted, was indeed a convinced and pugnacious Suarezian. On the genuine Thomist side Louis de Raeymaeker's *Philosophie de l'Etre* attains a real measure of achievement, and Etienne Gilson's *L'Etre et l'Essence* gives new life to the central question of being itself. Nevertheless the development of an adequate metaphysic can only be the result of co-operative effort, and much room still remains for a renewed scrutiny of the sources, especially of Aristotle and of Aquinas, and for an unremitting effort to preserve and to display continuity between the philosophy of being and the experience of being.

[1] Cf. E. Gilson, *L'Etre et l'Essence*, Paris, 1948, p. 168, n.

It might be supposed that the contemporary thinkers described as existentialists were making a contribution to the understanding of being. In fact, however, they are concerned with human existence and with the human situation rather than with being in general. *Existenz*, in the sense in which they use the term, is the fundamental dynamism of human nature as a source of thought and action. Hence, although some of what they say is relevant to the doctrine of substance, their main bias is towards psychology and ethics, and they have little to contribute to a metaphysic of being in general. For not only are we conscious of our own existence but we perceive the existence of other things, and it is the being which is common to persons and to things which is the subject of metaphysics.

2

A second and more radical cause of the contemporary neglect of metaphysics is to be found in the criticisms aimed at the possibility of such knowledge by Hume and Kant. More recent critics of the possibility of metaphysics have done little more than reformulate the difficulties raised by these two eminent thinkers. With Hume we need to notice both the limitations of the data which he accepted as genuinely given in experience and the limited scope which he assigned to reasoning from these data.

As a first approximation we may say that Hume rejected persistent data, such as the self, and acknowledged only the transitory data which he called impressions and ideas. There were sensations and the images derived from them; there were the reactions of feeling and the images of feelings. Nothing else seemed to Hume to be discoverable in experience or needed to account for it in any way in which we were capable of accounting for it. Of any alleged factor of a different sort we must always ask:

Whence shou'd it be deriv'd? Does it arise from an impression of sensation or of reflection? Point it out distinctly to us, that we may know its nature and qualities. But if you cannot point out *any such impression*, you may be certain you are mistaken, when you imagine you have *any such idea*.[1]

To describe summarily, then, what must be discussed in detail later, existence has no distinctive meaning. The notion of substance is dismissed; there is no impression of a permanent subject underlying the series of transient impressions which make up the history of a thing. Since Locke had reduced substance to an unknown somewhat with no function save that of unification, Hume was not without excuse in dispensing with so artificial a conception, although he would have been better advised to take note of Berkeley's rediscovery of the active self. Berkeley, however, is unduly brief and vague on this question, and Hume at any rate had no compunction in reducing experience to a succession of impressions and ideas. The identity which we attribute to the series of impressions which we should describe as belonging to the same thing is no more than a relation, even if it is an extremely puzzling relation.

Not only does Hume thus restrict the data of experience but his doctrine of relations is such as to reduce to very little the possibility of reasoning from original data. "Relations," says Hume, "may be divided into two classes; into such as depend entirely on the ideas, which we compare together, and such as may be chang'd without any change in the ideas."[2] Only relations of the former kind, which follow directly from the nature of their terms, can yield principles which are universal and certain and so afford a basis for deductive reasoning. Of such relations resemblance,

[1] Hume, *Treatise of Human Nature*, ed. Selby-Bigge, Oxford, 1928, bk. i, pt. 2, s. v, p. 65.
[2] *Human Nature*, bk. i, pt. 3, s. i, p. 69.

contrariety and degrees in quality are matters of immediate apprehension rather than of demonstration. There remain from Hume's list only proportions in quantity or number, whose fundamental principles are mathematical axioms. For Hume, therefore, the only valid deductive sciences are the mathematical.

Relations of the latter kind, which do not follow from their terms, can only be observed in experience. Such, according to Hume, are identity through time, relations of time and place, and causation. It is in vain that we seek any objectively necessary connection between what we call cause and what we call effect. For cause and effect are by definition distinct existents, and whatever things are conceived as distinct existents can be supposed to exist the one without the other. There can only be a psychological connection, in so far as repeated experience of similar sequences of events sets up habits of expectation. In what this psychological necessitation may consist Hume does not further enquire; he is content to have expelled the causal relation from the sphere which we instinctively, although in his opinion without rational justification, regard as an external world independent of the mind.

The Humian world, therefore, is not a world of persons and things but one of transitory atomic events. The connection of these events is in principle wholly unpredictable. Terms like being, substance and cause become almost or entirely meaningless. There is no room in such a world for a metaphysic or general science of being.

3

Hume, who was by no means without a sense of humour, did not suppose that the results of his philosophical reflections would be accepted by anyone as a satisfactory system for practical life. Indeed, in a famous passage, he professes his confidence that a change of occupation would at once dissipate the difficulties and doubts that he had aroused and would restore the ordinary assumptions of common sense. Nevertheless he was serious in putting his views forward as the inevitable conclusions of philosophical criticism. Hence, while on grounds of common sense we might feel ourselves entitled to assert that there is something wrong with Hume's thinking, it takes more than common sense to discover what is wrong. Common sense may serve as a rough negative criterion of the adequacy of a philosophical theory, but a positive philosophical construction demands a clearness and precision which transcends the level of mere common sense. Hume's is a challenge which has to be met on its own level of philosophical reflection.

Moreover, there are moments when it is possible to wonder whether Hume is not right after all and the rest is no more than vain words. To say that these are moments of intellectual fatigue is no insult to Hume, for it is literally true. We may deliberately make the experiment at any moment. Let us suppress as far as possible the activity of thinking and reduce our minds to a state of passive receptivity. We cannot altogether abolish mental activity or we should cease to be aware at all, but we can reduce it to a minimum. The more successful we are in this attempt, the more does experience take on the aspect attributed to it by Hume. Awareness of the self and of objects begins to fade away, and experience begins to seem a mere arbitrary succession of impressions without rational meaning or connection. So much for a deliberate effort to make Hume seem plausible, but it is when philosophers are tired and dispirited by the meagre results of mental activity that they are more usually tempted to believe that he may be right after all.

This is a clue to Kant's reaction against Hume. No doubt Kant had had misgivings about Wolff's confident dogmatism before he met with Hume, but what a reading of Hume crystallized in Kant's mind was the conviction that what Kant was to describe as categories of the understanding were

24

certainly not simply presented in experience in the same manner as acknowledged empirical data such as sense-qualities. On Hume's analysis such factors had to be dismissed, but Kant's advance beyond Hume consisted in the recognition that they were indispensable to human thought and made their appearance in the activity of thought itself. At the beginning of the *Critique of Pure Reason* the emphasis is more on the problem of the universal proposition than on the problem of the categories, but Kant's solutions of these problems are evidently interdependent, and there is a significant passage in the introduction to the second edition which appeals directly to a consideration of categorial thinking.

Not only in judgments but even in concepts is an *a priori* origin of some of them manifest. Eliminate gradually from your concept of a body all that is empirical, colour, hardness or softness, weight, even impenetrability; yet the space remains which the body, which has now faded away, once occupied, and that you cannot eliminate. Similarly, if you eliminate from your concept of any object, corporeal or incorporeal, all the qualities which are due to experience, you cannot cease to think of it as either a substance or dependent upon a substance (although this is a more determinate concept than that simply of an object). Hence, compelled by the necessity with which this concept forces itself upon you, you must admit that it resides in your *a priori* faculty of cognition.[1]

This is the converse of the kind of experiment in thinking which we described as making Hume seem plausible. Kant wants you to reduce as far as possible the passive and receptive element in thinking and so to lay bare what he regards as functions of the activity of thinking. Hume

[1] Kant, *Critique of Pure Reason*, Introduction to the Second Edition, sect. ii, B, 5–6.

had, then, asked a significant question. The philosopher cannot simply point out factors like substance or causality as he can indicate ordinary empirical qualities like yellowness or sweetness. Kant, whatever may be the value of his specific examples, may not have been far wrong in supposing that certain indispensable notions present themselves in the activity of thinking. Where he makes an arbitrary assumption is in holding that, because such factors appear in the activity of thinking, their validity is wholly dependent on and relative to our thinking. This must be called the great Kantian assumption, for, although it governs the whole of Kant's doctrine of the speculative reason, he never sees that it would need, and in fact lacks, justification.

In his treatment of the proposition Kant makes a similar modification of Hume's doctrine of relations but spoils his result by the same arbitrary assumption. Everyone who knows anything about Kant is familiar with his division of the kinds of judgment. In an analytic judgment the predicate is part of the meaning of the subject; in a synthetic judgment the predicate lies outside the meaning of the subject. A synthetic judgment is either *a posteriori*, when it is based upon experience, or *a priori*, when it is asserted as a deliverance of pure thinking. Kant was as well aware as Hume of the difficulties of inductive logic taken in isolation; a synthetic *a posteriori* judgment could never claim full universality or certainty. Hume had been content, as in the case of causal laws, to leave such judgments in an objectively dubious condition and had, if we may translate his teaching into Kantian terms, admitted only analytic judgments to possess *a priori* validity. Such is the effect of his contention that deductive reasoning is possible only with relations which are virtually contained in the meaning of their terms. That Hume and Kant differed about the status of mathematical propositions does not affect the more general relationship of their systems.

Here Kant's correction of Hume is to proclaim and to

vindicate the necessity of synthetic *a priori* judgments. Unless we admitted such principles of thought, we could not construct the body of knowledge that men have in fact constructed. Only by their means can we bestow order and consistency upon the material of experience. But the Kantian assumption affects judgments in the same way as it affects concepts. Because synthetic *a priori* judgments were necessities of thought, Kant held that their validity was wholly dependent on and relative to our thinking.

Our opposition to this assumption should not blind us to Kant's merit in singling out the question of the synthetic *a priori* judgment as cardinal to the possibility of metaphysics. His logic was not, of course, impeccable. He regarded the proposition as importing a mysterious identity of subject and predicate, and his discussion of the kinds of proposition is based on this inadequately clear view. If we reformulate his discussion in terms of a clearer logic, we realise that what he is talking about is the kind of compound proposition which we call an entailment. The question is not about a relation of subject and predicate but about a relation of predicates. If something is A, this or something else is B. If, *a priori* or apart from an inductive process, the only propositions which we were justified in asserting were what Kant called analytic, that would be equivalent to saying that the only entailments which we could assert were of the form: If something is AB, this is A. To extract A from an AB known at first only globally is not trivial, and the work of conceptual analysis is of the utmost importance in philosophy, but it is not the whole task. The possibility of fruitful inference depends on asserting entailments of the form: If something is A, this or something else is B, where B is not part of the analysis of A. Apart from his subjectivist assumption, therefore, what Kant did was to point out that the possibility of metaphysics depended on the validity of synthetic or informative as well as analytic or tautological entailments.

4

Philosophy has not, on the whole, succeeded in emancipating itself from Hume's restriction of experience and from Kant's subjectivist assumption. Since Kant's view that there is one and only one rational set of *a priori* categories and judgments is no longer generally accepted, philosophers tend to eke out the poverty of the Humian world by a changeable set of linguistic conventions. Words and other symbols are assigned the task of doing what Kant attributed to *a priori* thinking. Such is the outlook of those thinkers of today and yesterday whom we call logical positivists. For them, to describe a statement as metaphysical is one way of saying that it is nonsense.

Logical positivism is associated with the Vienna circle of logicians of twenty to thirty years ago, as well as with many English and American thinkers who found their doctrines congenial, but, since it is no longer held in its full rigour by many English philosophers, it will be convenient to refer to its tenets as maintained by a surviving member of the Vienna circle who recently republished his views. This is Richard von Mises, whose *Positivism*, a modified translation of his *Kleines Lehrbuch des Positivismus*, appeared in 1951. No recent English book has presented this type of outlook so candidly as well as so clearly and pleasantly.

The approach, as is common with our contemporaries, is through language. Since the distinctive status of thinking, as contrasted with sensing and imagining, is regarded as dubious, the specifically human contribution is made to consist in the creation of symbolic systems or languages. Hence our first criterion of a significant sentence or sequence of sentences is that it is in accordance with the rules which govern the use of words in the language to which it purports to belong. But, when we inquire about the things to which linguistic symbols are supposed to refer, we find at once that we are back at Hume's doctrine of experience, at any rate in the form in which it took new life in the work of the celebrated philosophical scientist Ernst Mach. Mach's elements or ultimate constituents of fact are essentially no other than Hume's impressions and ideas. We are not forbidden to use words like "body", "substance" and "thing", but we have to hold that they can be translated without remainder into terms of the elements. While they are a convenient shorthand for ordinary conversation, they have to be abandoned for purposes of exact investigation.

Besides empirical or factual sentences, which are finally translatable into sentences about elementary sensations and images, there are valid non-empirical sentences. These are the theorems of logic and mathematics, and their validity is due to their being "derived by *arbitrarily* fixed transformations of *arbitrarily* chosen basic assumptions."[1] It is in this sense that they are said to be tautologies. In other words, the rules of logic and mathematics are rules for the manipulation of symbols and are just as much a human creation as the symbols themselves. All logical and mathematical transformations are virtually contained in the basic assumptions which we have selected for such symbolic systems: we cannot get out of them more than we have put into them.

Many philosophers who are far from being Thomists, as well as many practising logicians and mathematicians, are unable to accept this conception of logic and mathematics as tautological. It seems too clear that, although symbols are in principle a matter of choice, how we can legitimately manipulate them depends not on us but on what we make them mean. The fact that two and two would not make four if "four" meant *five* does not entail that they can make anything but four as long as "four" means *four*, and this appears to tell us something about the real world which contains numerable groups of similar things. It is

[1] R. von Mises, *Positivism*, Harvard, 1951, p. 116.

comprehensible, however, that positivists should cling tenaciously to the view that valid non-empirical statements are tautological, for, if they surrendered it in any department of thought, who knows where they would be able to check the return of the *a priori*?

In the restoration of a critical metaphysic we have to try to show that, while our concepts must be derived from experience, pure thinking is then able to discern some necessary relationships between them. Nor shall we stop like Kant and regard such relationships as wholly dependent on and relative to the human faculty of thinking. We want to point out that the central notion of metaphysics, the notion of being, is one which both appears in the primary intellectual activity of the affirmation of existence and is the clue to the self-transcendence by which mind discovers itself in contact with reality. Since the positivist movement has lost its first fervour and subsists less as a militant doctrine than as a highly suspicious attitude on the part of contemporary philosophers to any attempt to transcend positivism, it should not be too much to ask them to suspend judgment on a matter which is neither evident nor proven and to be ready to accept contrary evidence if it can be produced.

The mention of evidence suggests another preliminary point, for we shall have to appeal for our principles to self-evidence. Metaphysical thinking is not a field of observation and experiment but of the analysis and synthesis of fundamental concepts. Many people feel the difficulty about the appeal to self-evidence, that it reduces to bare assertion. When I say that something is evident to me and you say that it is not evident to you, there seems to be nothing more to be said on either side and we do not appear to be either initiating or concluding a reasonable discussion. Besides, if anything is really self-evident, how can there possibly be a dispute about it? The facile answer is that at least one side must have misunderstood the terms. This is no doubt often the case, but we may feel misgiving about reducing the ultimate differences of opinion between philosophers to instances of verbal misunderstanding.

Whatever explanation we offer, we cannot dispense with the criterion of self-evidence. If we venture to assert anything at all, it must be either because we think this to be evident in itself or because we think we have sufficient extrinsic evidence for it. This evidence itself is either self-evidence or dependent on other evidence. If nothing were regarded in the end as self-evident, there could be no evidence of any sort.

It is possible, however, to mitigate the difficulty about self-evidence without rejecting the criterion. We can admit that it may be reasonable to dispute about what is self-evident even when we have a fair understanding of the terms, for the self-evident in the sense intended is what is simplest and most fundamental in the order of abstraction. But human knowledge does not really begin with the ultimate abstractions and gradually build itself up from them. Nor is it rational to say that it ought to do so, for it is never rational to combat a fact. Here lies the Cartesian error, for Descartes' method suggests that at some time we ought to throw all our preconceived ideas overboard and start afresh. C. S. Peirce had the answer to that when he said that "in truth, there is but one state of mind from which you can 'set out', namely, the very state of mind in which you actually find yourself at the time you do 'set out'—a state in which you are laden with an immense mass of cognition already formed, of which you cannot divest yourself if you would."[1]

But Peirce was mistaken if he thought that he had thus disposed of the Cartesian impulse in philosophy. For the great Cartesian contribution is that we must try as completely and as systematically as possible to penetrate beneath the surface of our commonsense convictions and thus to reach the abstractly self-evident principles on which these,

[1] C. S. Peirce, *Collected Papers*, ed. Hartshorne and Weiss, Harvard, 1931–35, vol. v, §416.

if they are legitimate, logically depend. It remains true, however, that what is evident in itself must be reached from what has become evident for us. Hence the establishment of first principles does not simply involve asking people to understand the terms and to inspect their connection; it has to include making clear that we could not know what we know ourselves to know unless we already implicitly accepted these principles. A conflict about what is self-evident need not be left as an opposition of incompatible assertions; it can and should lead to a fruitful discussion about the pre-suppositions of experience. A critical and constructive metaphysic ought to contain discussion of this kind.

CHAPTER II

The Problems of Being

I

W E MUST begin with the notion of being itself, and it
will not be surprising that this widest of all notions
has been the source of many difficulties and ambiguities. In
our own time, it is true, the attempt has been made to reduce
these difficulties to the level of linguistic ambiguity and to
evacuate their philosophical importance. We shall have to
show that this attempt has been unsuccessful, but it seems
better to begin by describing the problems in the way in
which they presented themselves in the history of thought.
When we have seen how philosophers have looked on these
problems, it will be easier to propose how to deal with them.
In this preliminary survey we shall allow the ambiguities
full play, for the ambiguities suggest the problems.

It appears to be the same to say that the opposite of being
is nothing and that being has no opposite. Heidegger has
tried to give a real meaning to nothingness, but this can
evidently be no more than a psychological meaning; nothingness is the ultimate source of dread. However poignant
Heidegger's meditations on this subject may be, they have
nothing to do with metaphysics. Ontologically nothing is
simply nothing. There seems to be a corollary that everything that we can think about is in some sense real. Yet this
makes the notion of reality thin almost to vanishing point.

For we think not only about what exists but also about
what does not exist, such as a centaur or a square circle.
Here again there is a difference. While a square circle is a

contradiction in terms, a centaur, even though it has no place in actual zoology, seems to have a certain conceivability or abstract possibility. We can certainly think about the possible in various senses. Beyond mere abstract conceivability there is what seems possible in relation to this or that set of circumstances. Does the invention of atomic weapons tend to bring about the end of human civilization or a general retreat from war on the grand scale? Both results are possible alternatives, but there is not much more that we can say at present. Moreover, there is the possible in the sense of what we are able to do or refrain from doing. I might take a holiday abroad next year, or I might be deterred by the necessary preliminary formalities and the exiguous financial allowance for foreign travel.

In both these types of case, both in what may possibly follow from a given situation and what an agent may possibly do, possibility takes shape in degrees of probability. With a wholly objective situation we are more inclined to make a definite estimate of the probabilities of its various possible outcomes; when our own action is involved, we assert our freedom by keeping our estimate more fluid. Yet our action is not so completely free that it is altogether exempt from calculations of probability, nor are many supposedly objective situations unaffected by the incalculable element of personal freedom. Probability, even if it is inevitably the guide of life, is equally inevitably an incompletely reliable guide. Yet probability is more than mere possibility, and even possibility is more than nothingness.

Another outcrop of reality manifests itself in the invention of fictions. To all right-minded readers of English Emma Woodhouse is as real as most of their acquaintance and considerably more real than most characters in history. No doubt she enjoys existence in the most literal and prosaic sense as a collection of marks on paper and of ideas in the minds of Jane Austen and her readers. But is that all? She is at least a projection from the mind of Miss Austen and can, through the medium of marks on paper, be similarly projected from the minds of readers. What is the ontological status of fictions?

There are other things that we normally speak of as real although their reality seems to be not quite on the same level as the primarily and undeniably real. We might instance powers and habits. A man is a rational being because he is capable of thinking, even though at the moment he is enjoying a dreamless slumber. Smith is really capable of driving a car because he has acquired the necessary habits of mind and body, even though at the moment he is peacefully occupying an armchair. Powers and habits seem to have a special kind of reality of their own, halfway between nonentity and full activity.

If all these things are going to be said to belong in some way to reality, it might seem that the metaphysician, aiming at the utmost generality, had to begin by trying to frame a concept of reality which would somehow cover the actual and the probable, the possible and the fictitious. But it would be rash to assume that any such concept could be framed. Moreover, all lesser concepts of reality evidently derive whatever significance they possess from the primary notion of existence. What is fully and unambiguously real is what exists. That we must eventually give some account of things about which we talk but which do not exist in the ordinary sense of the term is, no doubt, a philosophical duty, but it would be foolish to begin by involving ourselves in these embarrassments. The one comparatively plain and straightforward notion of being is that of existence, and it is with the fully real in this sense that we must make a start.

Another factor which has an evidently close connection with existence is individuality. For what really exists is fully and literally a *this*, an individual person or thing. When we are imagining or conceiving something possible or fictitious, we have in mind a collection of predicates, of qualities and activities, which might belong to a subject, but in such a case we know of no subject to which they do belong. Our supposal is precisely the projection from within ourselves of the shadow of an existent subject to which these attributes might belong, but the subject is a mere supposal; it is not affirmed really to exist. But the real existent is at the same time an individual subject of whatever attributes we know it to possess. All this calls for careful scrutiny, but so much is said here in order to specify the primary aspects of the problem of being as the problems of existence and of individuality.

2

Existence and individuality do not come to the fore in ancient philosophy. For existence becomes a problem when the possibility of non-existence is taken seriously. But contingency, or the possibility of non-existence, was not regarded as an ultimate fact by the Greek thinkers. They asked what was altogether real as opposed to the partially real or merely apparent, but they continued to cherish the hope that the world as a whole could eventually be exhibited as a manifestation of intelligible necessity. It was in the context of a theistic philosophy, a doctrine of creation, among the Jewish, Christian and Mohammedan thinkers of the Middle Ages, that the question of contingency, and, therefore, of existence, became acute.

It is not, perhaps, quite so obvious why the ancients should have had so little to say about individuality. Their comparative neglect of the factor of will, in which individual personality finds its fullest expression, had something to do with it. But, more than that, the concentration of Socrates and Plato on the discovery of universal essences, and Plato's conviction that such essences enjoyed a superior kind of reality to that possessed by the persons and things of the world of change and time, left individuality very much in the background. Even with Aristotle the species is considerably more prominent than its individual members.

36

In a theistic philosophy, in which a personal will is the source of the existence of precisely these individual persons and things and of no others, the problems of existence and individuality come into their own. Nor has the modern world forgotten these problems. Existence and contingency are even more puzzling for Heidegger on account of his comparative agnosticism and for Sartre on account of his atheism. No kind of philosophy could lay more stress on the individual than the existentialism of our own day. If we approach these problems in the medieval setting in which they arose, this does not mean that they are purely medieval problems with no contemporary significance.

The discussion of existence, then, emerges from an earlier condition of thought in which the existence of things is taken for granted and the problem of being is the problem of what really is as opposed to what is merely apparent, or of what is permanent as opposed to what is transitory. The earliest Greek philosophers looked for some permanent stuff out of which things were made and into which they were dissolved, and whose permanence made it in some sense more "real" than the things which were made out of it. So the Ionians, Thales finding the source of everything in water, Anaximenes in air, and Anaximander in some indeterminate substream. The contrast between the real and the merely apparent becomes explicit in the system of Parmenides; the way of truth discloses the real as a motionless homogeneous sphere altogether different from the busy world of various and changing things taken for granted by the way of opinion.

The type of problem remains the same for Plato although the answer is different. Real being belongs to the unchanging Forms; the world perceived by the senses is in a process of continuous becoming, as Heraclitus had already said, and so cannot lay claim to being in the full and proper meaning of the term. Even when, in the *Sophist*, Plato discusses the antithesis of being and not-being, it is to resolve not-being

37

into otherness. Not-being is not non-existence but charac-
terizes the situation in which A is said to be not-B, which
means that A is other than B. All being, then, participates
in identity and in otherness. This completely evades the
discussion of existence as opposed to non-existence.

We might expect more from Aristotle, for whom what
is primarily real is the concrete individual thing, first
substance. But the Aristotelian world is an uncreated world,
without beginning and without end, in which species
maintain themselves with relative necessity although their
members come into being and pass away. The problem for
Aristotle is not how individuals can be sufficiently alike to be
said to belong to the same species but how the specifically
identical form can be multiplied in the members of a species.
The problem of individuality is masked by the problem of
individuation, and the problem of contingency disappears
in a world which is necessary as a whole.

For the Neoplatonists the world is eminently capable
of interpretation as a fully intelligible system. No special
significance for our present subject need be attributed to the
view of Plotinus that the absolute, the One, is beyond being.
This is a simple consequence of the Platonic attribution of
real being to the Forms, which, in Plotinus's doctrine,
comprise the realm of the supreme intellect or *Nous*. But,
while the Forms thus make up an intelligible unity, this is a
unity in diversity which cannot be the absolute unity. The
unity of the absolute transcends the diversity of the Forms,
and so transcends being in the sense in which being is
proper to the Forms.

This Neoplatonic conviction, however, that absoluteness
and metaphysical simplicity are convertible terms, is not
irrelevant to our subject, for it implies an explanation of
finiteness and dependence by means of metaphysical
composition, a distinction and tension of principles of being
within the finite thing. The Aristotelian theory of hylomorphism, the composition of matter and form, filled this

need as far as corporeal things were concerned. But hylomorphism could not be a general explanation of finiteness and dependence unless the highly artificial doctrine of a spiritual hylomorphism, a composition of *materia spiritualis* and *forma spiritualis* in incorporeal beings, was accepted, as it was accepted by some thirteenth-century philosophers. St. Thomas and others who rejected this unintelligible doctrine found the explanation in a composition of *essentia* and *esse*, and their discussions of this question involved an analysis of the meaning of existence.

The fundamental thought here is that the simple just is what it is and cannot be otherwise, whereas, in the case of anything in which there is a distinction of real factors, it is always possible and indeed necessary to ask how their union was brought about. This is maintained even when, in the case of principles of being which are not independent existents, they can have no reality except in union with each other. For, although they did not pre-exist, their union is as much a fact as what they intrinsically are and is a sign that the composite thing which they make up calls for causal explanation.

Metaphysicians have often been tempted to begin by setting up some such principle of the compositeness of the finite and contingent and thence to deduce its consequences. But this order of procedure seems somewhat unreal, for the significance of the terms involved is scarcely evident in pure abstraction. Until they are seen to be instantiated and are considered in their instantiation, one cannot avoid a doubt whether they are meaningful or not. Hence we do better by beginning with an analysis of existence as it appears in experience, but it is well to remember that the doctrine of the metaphysical composition of the finite and contingent has influenced the way in which the problem of existence has come to be presented in the history of thought.

3

To exist is a verb, and it can be treated grammatically like any other intransitive verb. Do horses exist? Yes, horses exist. Do unicorns exist? No, unicorns do not exist. Do dodos exist? No, they existed but they no longer exist. It might seem that there was no more mystery about existence than there is about any other predicate and that, just as some things have tails and some have not, so some have existence and some have not.

This naïve way of dealing with existence is characteristic of the Mohammedan philosopher Avicenna, who develops ideas already to be found in Al Farabi. If by essence we understand *what* a thing is, i.e. everything about it except the fact *that* it is, which is its existence, we may say that there are three states of essence. Absolutely and in itself, apart from any kind of existence or realization, the essence is neither individual nor universal. An essence receives a logical existence or realization in the mind and is here universal; the essence of horse, as entertained by the mind, is a predicate applicable to all horses. But, when an essence receives real existence, it is always individual; it is this horse or that horse. The bare essence is merely in a state of possibility; it is transferred to the plane of actuality by the reception of existence. Hence, in the case of any contingent being, there is a distinction between essence and existence, and existence appears as a kind of "accident" of essence. Avicenna does not, of course, mean that existence is an accident in the proper Aristotelian sense, for the existence of a substance clearly pertains to the category of substance, but it is predicated accidentally of any contingent subject.

With this doctrine of existence we may compare the view implicit in the ontological argument of St. Anselm. St. Anselm says in effect that we must acknowledge the existence of God in order to think of him without contradiction, for the essence of infinite being entails its existence. By contrast, then, existence is not entailed by the essence of finite being and must, if we use the language of Avicenna, be predicated accidentally of it.

The difficulty in accepting this account as philosophically adequate becomes evident when we begin to think about things which do not exist, like unicorns and the present Tsar of Russia. If a thing does not exist, what is there which can receive existence? If we are really going to say that a finite essence is first possible and then becomes actual by receiving existence, it seems that it must already "exist" in some curious way in the state of possibility. Then, when it actually comes to exist, what really begins to "exist" would not be the thing but rather its existence. An essence which already "exists" in one sense as a possible thing and an existence in another sense which begins to "exist" when the thing becomes actual can scarcely be regarded as an intelligible combination, for it is impossible to find distinct meanings for these two uses of existence. To alter the word and to speak of possibilities as subsisting would only be to invent a name without a meaning. And the one subject of which it is logically impossible to predicate existence is existence itself, just as it is absurd to say that blueness is blue.

All these difficulties arise from trying to talk of a world composed both of things that exist and of things that do not exist. What we need in order to see that there is something seriously wrong with the Avicennian ontology is the simple acknowledgment that the world consists only of things that exist. Nevertheless we may well suspect that Avicenna, and Anselm too, were trying awkwardly and unsuccessfully to say something that ought to be said about the contrast of the contingent and the necessary, the finite and the infinite. The development of a more appropriate mode of utterance takes us to St. Thomas Aquinas.

4

Already in the generation before Aquinas some Western thinkers, like William of Auvergne, had adopted the Avicennian distinction of essence and existence as a mode of characterizing the finite in its contrast with the infinite. In the earliest summary of his principles, the opusculum *De Ente et Essentia*, St. Thomas himself has some sentences which are wholly Avicennian, although he goes on to indicate a new way of looking at the question. He says, first, that we can understand what a thing is, such as a man or a phoenix, without knowing whether such a thing actually exists. Hence existence does not belong to the essence of a finite thing, but comes from outside and enters into composition with it.[1] Here the mental picture, as with Avicenna, is of an essence enjoying some sort of ontological status as a possibility and then receiving actual existence from a cause, and, as before, we want to ask what a thing can possibly be if it does not yet exist.

When, however, we come to the other term of comparison, absolute being, we find that it is not presented by St. Thomas as an essence which entails its existence and which, consequently, cannot be conceived except as including existence; it is presented as *ipsum esse subsistens*, subsistent being itself. Evidently we can no longer translate *esse* as existence, for subsistent existence is a meaningless phrase; existence is always the existence of something. *Esse* must now be translated as being in its fullest sense, including in itself all that is positive in the notion of essence; *essentia*, in so far as it is contrasted with *esse* as now understood, becomes a mere principle of limitation or finiteness, making being into the being of this or that limited kind of thing.

Thus, in the *De Ente et Essentia* itself, God, as *esse subsistens*, is declared to possess all the perfections of every kind

[1] St. Thomas Aquinas, *De Ente et Essentia*, cap. 5 (or 3).

of being in a transcendent unity.[1] In the same way the *Summa Theologica* argues the infinite perfection of God from the fact that he is subsistent being.[2] In the *Summa contra Gentiles* the distinction of *essentia* and *esse* in finite things is based on the argument that, where there is no such distinction, *esse* must be subsistent and, therefore, infinite.[3]

In this perspective it is plain that there is no positive essence awaiting the reception of existence. The finite thing is not composite because it is first an essence and then receives existence; it is composite because it is participated and limited being. If we think in terms of the older dichotomy of positive essence and bare existence "it would be much more correct to speak of the essence of an existence than to speak . . . of the existence of an essence",[4] for *what a thing is* is the specification of its *being*.

St. Thomas, then, was saying something very different from Avicenna's doctrine, but he seems to have been content to leave it to others to notice his originality. That not all have noticed it is the reason why a certain ambiguity has infected the discussion of *essentia* and *esse* ever since. Are we talking, in the manner of Avicenna, about the relationship of a positive essence and a bare existence or, in accordance with the personal thought of St. Thomas, about a principle of positive being and a principle of limitation? Far too much controversial ink has been spilt by writers who have omitted this preliminary consideration of terms.

Two years after St. Thomas's death Giles of Rome composed his *Theoremata de Esse et Essentia*. In this work he maintained that *essentia* and *esse* in finite things are distinct as *res* and *res*. He met from most of his contemporaries with a violent opposition which St. Thomas's doctrine had not evoked. Nor is this to be wondered at. He seems to have understood his terms in the Avicennian manner and, even

[1] *De Ente et Essentia*, cap. 6 (or 4).
[2] St. Thomas Aquinas, *Summa Theologica*, I, q. 4, a. ii.
[3] St. Thomas Aquinas, *Summa contra Gentiles*, II, cap. 52.
[4] E. Gilson, *God and Philosophy*, Yale, 1941, p. 69 n.

on a Thomistic interpretation, would have been guilty of crudity and exaggeration. For there is only one thing (*res*), composed though it may be on the metaphysical level of principles of being and of limitation. Opposition to the Aegidian distinction of essence and existence does not entail opposition to St. Thomas, but the dust raised by the controversial ardour of Giles and his opponents contributed to clouding the issue.

5

So far there had not been full discussion of individuality in general. The problem of *individuation*, of the multiplication of members of a species, had received much attention, but this is a different question in which the notion of *individuality* is taken for granted. It is not our business to deal with it, since it belongs to the philosophy of the material world and not to general metaphysics.

Duns Scotus was the first to assert clearly that, whatever the conditions of individuality may be, the notion of individuality is itself primary and irreducible. *Haecceitas est de se haec*. Thisness is of itself this; it must be known in itself and for itself before anything else can be said about it. When this has once been stated, it seems to be quite undeniable. There is no possible definition of thisness or individuality in general; we have to learn what it means by practice. Unfortunately Scotus does not seem to have much more to tell us about it. It may well be that, when we have a complete critical text of his works, we shall have to revise this estimate, but the conception of Scotus's doctrine at present available to the practising philosopher offers no further help on the subject.

For, when we look at the rest of Scotus's metaphysical system, he seems to be primarily a logician for whom the ontological order must be exactly parallel to the logical order. Where a significant logical distinction can be made, there must be some kind of real or, as he says, formal distinction. The logical structure of the notes comprising the nature of a thing is matched by a distinction of formalities in the real order. In the last resort, therefore, a thing as envisaged by Scotus appears to be not unlike a bundle of universals tied together by thisness, and that is not a very plausible or helpful view. Once again, however, we are on the threshold of a genuine problem. It can hardly be doubted that individuality is an irreducible factor in the analysis of being, but it is not wholly disconnected from other factors, nor can it be arbitrarily applied. The connection of reality and individuality is a matter to be explored.

To sum up, therefore, we have tried in this chapter to indicate the central problems of being with some reference to their historical origin. In the logical order it is one thing to say what a thing is and another to say that it exists, but to transfer this distinction without modification into the real order in the manner of Avicenna or Giles of Rome leads to insuperable difficulties. St. Thomas offers a more searching discrimination, but the notion of a real principle of pure limitation is not without its difficulties either. There is evidently an intimate connection between individuality and reality, but we have not yet seen how this connection is to be explained. It is with these points in mind that we should embark on our own analysis of being in terms of that experience of being which is both the immediate awareness and the primary judgment of existence.

CHAPTER III

The Analysis of Being

I

THE affirmation of existence is both logically and ontologically elementary. Whatever else we may assert of anything, whatever quality or activity we attribute to it, we presuppose that it exists and that we and those with whom we are communicating know that it exists. Reflecting on the logical aspect of the affirmation of existence, we find in its fundamental inevitability the guarantee that knowing and being are essentially in touch. All the difficulties about what we know and how we know it cannot upset the fundamental orientation of knowing to being. At present, however, it is on the ontological aspect of the affirmation of being that we want to dwell.

When we affirm that something exists, we are using existence as a grammatical and logical predicate. The usage is linguistically quite natural. It is perfectly sound English to say that cats and tigers exist and that unicorns and centaurs do not exist. Nor does the logical analysis of this grammatical usage present any insuperable difficulty, although it involves giving to *exist* an unexpectedly complex meaning. Of what do we assert existence when we say that cats exist? It is clear that we have in mind a collection of notes which together make up a distinctive description, or what we take to be a distinctive description, of the kind of animal which we call a cat. Not every one will have exactly the same description in mind, and the zoologist, for example, will be thinking of something considerably more precise than the ordinary man's description, but this is not really embarrassing, for a thing can have more than one distinctive description.

Some distinctive description of a cat is, therefore, the logical subject of our thought, and, when we say that cats exist, the predicate *exists* is equivalent to *having a counterpart in fact*. To affirm that cats exist is to affirm that our distinctive description of a cat has real instances corresponding with it. If we use the term *essence* to cover all the descriptive notes which can be applied to anything, we have a term which is exclusive only of existence, and we may say that the logical analysis of the existential proposition has presented us with a logical relationship of essence as subject and existence as predicate in the senses indicated.

We might then be tempted to transfer this analysis from the logical to the real order and to say that real things consist of essences possessing existence. But it is at once evident that this is not a simple and unambiguous transposition, for the term *existence* has changed its meaning. It has now reacquired its ordinary and undefinable meaning instead of its logical significance of having a counterpart in fact. A real existent cat is a cat which exists in the ordinary meaning of the word.

This should be enough to warn us against an over-simplified doctrine of the correspondence of the logical with the real, but there is another almost equally obvious difficulty. Essence and existence, in the senses in which we have hitherto used them, are abstractions. Being furry and having whiskers and eating mice and birds, and anything else that comes to mind when we try to describe a cat, are attributes which together apply to all cats and severally apply to things other than cats as well. They are universal concepts, and so is existence as we have hitherto thought of it, for it is the bare notion of existence which applies indifferently to everything that exists. But real things are not simply bundles of abstractions, collections of universals;

reality is not, in Bradley's famous phrase, "some spectral woof of impalpable abstractions or unearthly ballet of bloodless categories". Real things are individual; each is a this or a that, and thisness and thatness are irreducible to universal terms.

Hence, if we wanted to construct an ontology which departed as little as possible from our logical analysis, we should nevertheless have to botch our scheme once again. We should have to say that things consisted of essences endowed with existence and constituted as particulars. Our distinction of essence and existence would correspond with that made by Avicenna and, perhaps, by Giles of Rome, and we should have progressed beyond them by recognizing with Duns Scotus the irreducible character of thisness. Even so our difficulties would be by no means at an end, and further reflection compels us to make a much more radical transformation.

2

Discussion among contemporary British philosophers begins with Bertrand Russell's resolute attempt to dispose of the problem of being by reducing it to a mere linguistic confusion. According to Russell, "we may correctly say 'men exist', meaning that 'x is a man' is sometimes true". And "this is the fundamental meaning of the word 'existence'"; it refers primarily and properly not to singulars but to propositional functions. A propositional function is what remains of a proposition when the subject is left indeterminate. "Socrates is a man" is a proposition, but "x is a man" is a propositional function. If we generalize the predicate also as φ, the form of a propositional function becomes "x is φ" or φx. Hence "'terms satisfying φx exist' means 'φx is sometimes true'; but 'a exists' (where a is a term satisfying φx) is a mere noise or shape devoid of significance". Thus Russell reduces the meaning of existence to a matter of the truth-value of propositional functions, and he adds that "it will be found by bearing in mind this simple fallacy we can solve many ancient philosophical puzzles concerning the meaning of existence".[1]

This is a very queer doctrine indeed, for what is the meaning of "φx is sometimes true"? Where a definite or exclusive description, such as "the author of *Waverley*", is involved, Russell puts it reasonably enough that "the term satisfying the function φx exists" means "There is a term c such that φx is always equivalent to 'x is c'".[2] Where φ is a general term or class-concept, if we are to affirm that φx is sometimes true in the logical sense of "some" in which it means "at least one", we must presumably say that "φx is sometimes true" means "There is at least one term c such that c is φ". But now the verb "to be" has come back naked and unashamed.

It is really only too evident that we cannot say that some men exist unless we know that at least one man exists; that is, we must know first that Socrates or Plato, or Tom or Dick or Harry, exists. So far is the fundamental meaning of existence from applying to propositional functions that, unless we knew that individuals existed, the term would have no meaning at all. It is difficult to see any reason why Russell denies meaning to "Socrates exists" except that, if "Socrates" is really the name of something, it follows necessarily that Socrates exists. If Russell wants to say that, in consequence, "exists" adds nothing to "Socrates", he is forgetting that terms are abstractions and that the fundamental unit of knowledge is the judgment. That, after all, is the reason why he made an advance in logic by speaking of propositional functions instead of amputated predicates. But a subject is equally incomplete in meaning without a predicate. If the significance of "man" as a possible predicate is properly expanded in the predicative propositional function "x is a man", so the significance of "Socrates" as a possible subject is properly expanded in what may be

---

[1] B. Russell, *Introduction to Mathematical Philosophy*, London, 1919, pp. 164–5.
[2] *Introduction*, pp. 177–8.

called a subjective propositional function "Socrates is φ".
To say "Socrates" without anything else expressed or understood is not to state anything. And the logically fundamental
proposition about Socrates is that Socrates exists. This
represents our primary awareness of a fact of experience,
and the "ancient philosophical puzzles concerning the
meaning of existence" subsist in their entirety.

More recent comment has, on the whole, harked back
either to Russell's logic or to Kant's denial that existence is
a genuine predicate, of which more in a moment. In an
early paper Professor Ryle supplemented Kant by pointing
out how many quasi-ontological predicates demanded to be
treated in the same way but made the arbitrary addition
that, if being was not a genuine predicate, it was equally
ineligible as a subject.[1] Mr. W. Kneale recognized that "the
fundamental thesis of those who believe existence to be a
predicate is that there is a sense of 'being' logically prior to
existence and applicable to the possible as well as to the
actual" but was content with the main lines of Russell's
disposal of the problem.[2] Professor G. E. Moore agreed that
Russell had revealed one way of talking about existence but
held with common sense that there was another legitimate
way of talking about existence in which it was applicable to
singulars.[3] Nothing very conclusive emerges from these
papers, and it is clear that we must go back at least as far as
Kant to appreciate the significance of discussions of the
meaning of existence since his time.

3

Descartes had reduced the ontological argument of St.
Anselm for the existence of God, very variously judged

[1] G. Ryle, "Systematically Misleading Expressions", in *Proceedings of the Aristotelian Society*, 1931–2, pp. 143–50.
[2] W. Kneale, "Is Existence a Predicate?", in *Arist. Soc. Supp. Vol.*, 1936, pp.
154–74.
[3] G. E. Moore, ibid., pp. 175–88.

in the Middle Ages and since, to its simplest form. For Descartes the very idea of a perfect being included the note of existence; to think of it as non-existent was to think of it as less than perfect. In the logical sense in which we have so far spoken of essence and existence the essence of a perfect being implied its existence. Hence to think of a perfect being without affirming its existence was to fall into contradiction. To think clearly of God involved affirming that God existed. The argument in this form satisfied Descartes.

Kant's objection is summed up in the statement that existence is not a real predicate.[1] Whatever may be legitimate in grammar or in logic, a real subject is really presupposed to anything that is attributed to it. The ontological argument purports to infer the divine existence from the divine essence. If the argument were to be valid, God's essence would have to be really prior in nature to his existence. But this is absurd. Nothing can be prior to the existence of anything. If it does not exist, it is nothing at all and there is nothing to which existence can be really attributed.

Consider the case, says Kant, of a hundred dollars which may or may not exist; you may or may not possess a hundred dollars. There is in this case no real common subject of which existence or non-existence can be indifferently predicated. If the hundred dollars exist, then there are indeed a hundred real dollars, but, if you deny their existence, you are not merely denying one attribute among many but are negating the whole subject. When you say that the hundred dollars do not exist, you are not speaking of a hundred dollars which are real in some Pickwickian sense but happen not to exist; you can be speaking only of an idea of a hundred dollars to which nothing corresponds in fact. Hence there is no real subject prior to existence, and existence is not a real predicate. To attempt to infer existence from essence is to treat essence as the subject of existence. But this is a

[1] Kant, *Kritik der reinen Vernunft*, "Von der Unmöglichkeit eines ontologischen Beweises vom Dasein Gottes", A 592–602, B 620–30.

contradiction, for it makes essence in itself both real and not real. Consequently the ontological argument, which proceeds in this way, is invalid.

All this is clear enough, although, if Kant had used the modern logic of entailment, he might have arrived at his point more rapidly. The ontological argument asserts that the divine essence entails existence. But a relation of entailment is, in the first place, a relation between two propositional functions such that, if an instance of the former occurs, there will be an instance of the latter also. That colour entails extension means that, if anything is coloured, it is extended. Hence the principle of the ontological argument can be expanded in the form that, if the divine essence exists, its existence exists. It is evidently meaningless to speak of the existence of existence, and, in general, it is evident that there cannot be a relation of entailment between essence and existence. To suppose that there can is a glaring instance of that reification of abstractions to which philosophers are liable. No doubt the principle of the ontological argument can be more charitably interpreted as meaning that, if God exists, he exists necessarily, but this allows no inference to the actual existence of God, which has to be established on more solid grounds than a mere manipulation of concepts.

Nevertheless, if we go back to Kant's manner of speaking, he has said something true and important in stating that in the real order there is no subject prior to existence and susceptible either of existence or of non-existence. Since Kant's purpose was simply to explode the ontological argument, he left the matter there, but we want to use his conclusion as a stepping-stone to a more adequate view of being. The point at which we have now arrived is that, in penetrating through the logical to the real order, we have to think not of an essence possessing existence but rather of existence taking shape in an essence. To speak of existence as an ultimate subject is not altogether appropriate, for existence is an abstraction, but it is clear that in the real order existence is more like the subject of essence than essence is like the subject of existence.

4

The next point to notice is that the notion of being cannot be detached from the forms which being takes but that these are forms of being and being enters intrinsically into them. Not only are beings alike precisely as being but their differences also belong to being. This is recognized by Aristotle where he says that being is not a genus, for a true generic notion can be isolated from its specific differences and is not attributed to them, whereas being must be attributed to all the different modes of being.[1] Hence the categories represent different senses of being itself.[2] St. Thomas explains Aristotle's doctrine in the following way.

If being were a genus, some difference would have to be found in order to specify it; but no difference participates in its genus in the sense that the genus is an element in it; for thus the genus would appear twice in the definition of the species. A difference must then be outside the meaning of the genus. But nothing can be outside what is meant by being; hence being cannot be specified by any difference. It follows, therefore, that being is not a genus.[3]

The contrast made here, apart from the technical terms of Aristotelian logic, is between a notion which is closed and determinate and one which is open and indeterminate. Aristotle required generic and differential notions to be, as notions, closed and determinate although, as factors in the structure of reality, they were related as determinable to determinant. This is not the moment to criticize the some-

---

[1] Aristotle, *Metaphysics*, B, 3, 998b, 22.
[2] *Metaphysics*, Δ, 7, 1017a, 22.
[3] St. Thomas Aquinas, *Summa contra Gentiles*, I, 25.

what artificial character of Aristotle's theory of classification; it is enough to observe that there are such closed and determinate notions, whether they are capable of doing the job that Aristotle assigns to them or not. To take the kind of example that Aristotle had in mind, it is one thing to be an animal and quite another to be rational; the meaning of animal is altogether outside the meaning of rational, although in man, as a rational animal, animal is related to rationality as genus to specific difference.

Being, however, is not an isolable factor in this sense, and the modes of being are not extrinsic to it. They are intrinsic differentiations of being, and being overflows into them and becomes determinate in them. Logically we can distinguish the bare fact of existence from the forms of being which are summed up under the name of essence; when we think of what being really is, we cannot distinguish it from the forms which it takes and which are themselves being. Being covers all that is positive in everything that is.

Yet our experience is not simply of a vast ocean of being; it is an experience of distinct and different things. But, if being is as we have described it, what is left to differentiate one thing from another? Only, we must begin by saying, what it is not. The limits within which each participates being are what make one finite thing different from another. Consequently, if we are to be true to the multiplicity revealed by experience and not to say that everything is really one, we must admit two antithetical but complementary factors in every finite thing, a principle of being and a principle of limitation. These seem to be what St. Thomas came in the end to mean by *esse* and *essentia*.

This doctrine is not susceptible to the obvious objection raised by an alleged distinction between a positive essence and a bare existence which it might be said to receive and to enjoy. Such a view is open to precisely the same kind of objection as the ontological argument. It supposes that there is a common subject of existence and non-existence and that essence has some kind of reality apart from existence. That this is nonsense we have already pointed out, but it is not what is asserted by the Thomistic distinction of *esse* and *essentia*.

Nevertheless, since there has been so much confusion on the question, it would seem highly desirable to make some difference of terminology. We can hardly alter St. Thomas's own Latin terminology without a permission which his death some seven centuries ago precludes him from giving, but we might at least find unambiguous English terms. In English, at any rate, *essence* can hardly be deprived of a positive meaning and *existence* usually just means existence. Hence we might reserve *essence* and *existence* for the logical distinction between what is and the bare fact that it is. *Being*, as contrasted with bare existence, is excellently adapted to convey to the English mind the full richness and positivity of the modes of being. It is more difficult to find an appropriate name for St. Thomas's principle of limitation. Perhaps the word *quiddity*, which is no longer in common use even among philosophers, might be artificially reserved for this purpose. Let us say, therefore, that what Thomism asserts in every finite thing is a metaphysical tension of being and quiddity.

5

There remains, however, a serious objection which can be brought against the Thomistic distinction in its proper meaning. Is there not a contradiction in making a mere principle of limitation into a positive factor in the constitution of finite being? A limitation is a negation and nothing more. To assert a positive principle of limitation is like asserting that the surface of a sphere is distinct from the sphere itself. That is clearly nonsense, and so, therefore, it will be said, is the Thomistic conception of *essentia* or quiddity.

I do not think that Thomists have ever given an adequate answer to this objection. To say that quiddity is not a thing but only a metaphysical principle of being is not enough, for it must have its own kind of positivity if it is to be anything at all. The problem is to provide it with positivity without encroaching upon the positivity of being. Thomists have relied upon demonstrating the necessity of such a principle in order to account for the distinction and difference of things. The argument is a sound one and deserves respect even if it lands us in an insoluble mystery. But it is up to the metaphysician to make the conclusion less mysterious if he can.

Here I proceed on my own responsibility and call attention to a factor which is not much emphasized in the Thomist tradition. This is the factor of individuality or thisness. A generation after St. Thomas, Duns Scotus pointed out the irreducibility of thisness, and reflection shows him to have been justified in doing so. Everything that exists, no doubt, is individual, but the character of individuality is clearest in those things of which our knowledge is most intimate, our fellow-men. Now it is one thing to have even the fullest possible information about a man and another to know the man himself, for in knowing the man himself we are acquainted with the indefinable individuality or thisness of which his qualities and activities are a manifestation. At the same time we are not acquainted with individuality apart from qualities and activities; apart from these it becomes a general notion, although evidently of a unique kind, applicable to any individual. Acquaintance with a man in the concrete is neither awareness of his bare individuality nor knowledge of the sum of his qualities and activities but a grasp in some measure of the inseparable real unity of his individuality with his qualities and activities.

Individuality is a positive factor but it is not on the same level as the qualities and activities which, in the abstract, might be possessed by many individuals. In its own right it is an irreducible factor, but it is not an unrelated addition to the being of things. When we reflect on finite individuality, we see that it is precisely the unique mould within which each thing participates being. Hence we must finally identify it with what St. Thomas came to mean by *essentia* or quiddity. In this way individuality both finds its appropriate place in the metaphysical analysis of finite being and also, since it has its own unique kind of positivity, dissipates the mystery which would surround a principle of pure limitation. It is a positive principle in its own right but a principle of the limitation or participation of being. Boethius seems to have divined something of this when he said *Diversum est esse et id quod est*, distinguishing the finite subject (*id quod est*) from the *esse* which it participates.[1]

Beginning, therefore, from the plain logical distinction between what exists and its existence, we found that we could not transpose this distinction without modification on to the ontological level, for existence is not a real predicate or attribute. There is no common subject of existence and non-existence. Taking existence, then, as primary, we found that on the ontological level this was an open notion expanding into and including all the modes of being. Thus the logical concept of bare existence was replaced by the ontological notion of being. The differences between finite things had, consequently, to be explained by a principle of non-being or limitation. That this could be a positive principle became intelligible when it was identified with the unique factor of individuality, which possesses a positivity of its own on a level different from the being which individuals variously participate. That is, indeed, how we are aware of other things when we know them in their singularity. They are this or that endowed with their various measures of being, just as we are conscious of ourselves as unique selves possessing our own measure of being. The test of our own consciousness is the final proof that our analysis of being has not been a mere manipulation of words or concepts. Reflection reveals to us a unique self which is at the same time the

[1] Boethius, *De Hebdomadibus*, ch. ii.

measure of our participation in the being in which all things share.

There is, then, a distinction between the logical and the real order. To think ontologically we have had to criticize and to modify the natural processes of human logic. The reason is that for the most part our knowledge is receptive. In knowing things other than ourselves we must first be affected by them and then provide the matter of our conceptual assimilation with a factual reference. In doubtful cases we are obliged to linger among concepts and to ask whether there is anything in fact corresponding with them. But factual reference, whether certain or doubtful, would be impossible unless we were unambiguously acquainted with the fact of our own reality. Self-consciousness is always an ontological form of thinking. Nevertheless so many of our habits of thought are derived from our way of knowing the external world that a critical metaphysic, as we shall see, has constantly to be making a distinction between the logical and the real order.

Chapter IV

Distinction and Relatedness

I

So far, in speaking of existence, we have considered the ontological counterpart of what in the logical order is the existential judgment. Just as the existential judgment involves the unity in distinction of *what* is and the fact *that* it is, so the analysis of finite being as presented to us in experience involves a distinction in unity, but it turns out to be a different distinction. Ontological analysis reveals a distinction of being and individual quiddity within the unity of the thing.

Distinction and relatedness are thus fundamental both to our thinking about things and to the things about which we think. From the primary recognition of existence our thinking proceeds farther *dividendo et componendo*, as the ancient phrase has it. There seems to be no limit to possible discriminations and possible kinds of discrimination and, correspondingly, no limit to possible relationships and possible kinds of relationship. The difficulty now is to find some principle of order which will integrate the structure of thinking and exhibit the structure of fact.

A certain choice is inevitable at this point, but it is not an arbitrary choice. We want not only to discover distinctions and relations which are really there but to arrive at a framework of thought which manifests fact in due proportion and significance. It is a question, as Emile Meyerson put it in his work *Du Cheminement de la Pensée*, of discovering *la fibre*, of finding the thread which will best lead us through the labyrinth of reality. To discriminate men as either red-headed or not red-headed is a perfectly valid classification, but for most purposes it is not of great importance. The importance which it assumes in the Sherlock Holmes story of *The Red-Headed League* is one which we easily see to be both adventitious and fictitious. Many equally trivial principles of unity and distinction could be cited or supposed, and it is one of the relatively utilitarian justifications of an attempt to think philosophically that it is a deterrent to such forms of triviality.

European thought has mainly been dominated or goaded into revolt, but not less obsessed when goaded into revolt, by Aristotle's general scheme of distinction and relation. A large part of what the average man would describe as common sense is fossilized Aristotle. It is when we study Oriental philosophies that we cannot help seeing that what is common sense for the European is not common sense for everybody. We have to divest ourselves of our customary categories in order genuinely to think ourselves into the atmosphere of Hindu or Chinese philosophy. Here we might be expected to make the great surrender. We might be expected either to admit that all metaphysical frameworks are equally valid or to propose some new scheme for the metaphysics of the future. If, nevertheless, we assert that the Aristotelian scheme does provide us with the thread through the labyrinth and that the relative clarity and sobriety of European thought owes more than it realises to the pioneering genius of Aristotle, it is with a full awareness that alternative schemes of thought are possible. This awareness alone redeems the assertion from being merely banal or conventional and makes it a proposition which can be, and deserves to be, tested in practice.

A consequence of this element of choice, however, is that alternative approaches may be complementary rather than mutually exclusive. Ideally, of course, the perfect philosophy could and would harmonize everything of value that philosophers have ever put forward, and the genuine philosopher tries, wherever possible, to understand and to make use of what his fellows were driving at rather than to refute and reject them. Nevertheless the process of assimilation and harmonization is slow and difficult. That is why a study of the whole history of philosophy is necessary in order to obtain any adequate appreciation of the richness of philosophical experience. A vague and arbitrary eclecticism, of course, would be just as undesirable as a pedantic rejection of all unfamiliar ways of approach. We must try to offer a positive doctrine which is yet open to development and capable of assimilation. So much, then, by way of reflection on the general character of analytic thinking before we proceed to details.

2

In the *Sophist* Plato considers the difficulties arising from the notion of not-being. It seems to be a glaring contradiction to say that not-being is, yet we do not seem to be able to describe the world adequately without taking into account what things are not as well as what they are. Plato's answer is that we do not have to suppose the being of absolute not-being or nothingness; the not-being which enters into the constitution of the real world is relative not-being or otherness. Our need of not-being is precisely the need of making distinctions.

The kinds of distinction are, then, the kinds of otherness that come to our notice. Now Plato already remarked that, while being is manifold, not-being is infinite, for everything that is is other than everything else actual or possible.[1] The kinds of distinction are innumerable, and any attempt at classification must be selective, aiming at that distinction of distinctions which is most useful for thinking clearly about the world.

Thomists are in the habit of discriminating real and logical distinctions, and a logical distinction may be with or

[1] Plato, *Sophist*, 256, E.

without a foundation in fact. A logical distinction without a foundation in fact has no relevance to ontology, for it would be more clearly described as a purely verbal distinction. "Sir Winston Churchill" and "The present Prime Minister of Great Britain", in so far as these phrases designate a concrete person and are not thought of as distinct operations of naming, designate the same person. The distinction between Sir Winston Churchill and the present Prime Minister of Great Britain is purely verbal. The conception, however, of a logical distinction with a foundation in fact raises a question. For what sort of foundation in fact can a distinction have unless this is some sort of distinction in fact? It might seem that, if we made a distinction in thought where there is no distinction in fact, we should merely be thinking wrongly. Hence every justifiable distinction which was not purely verbal would be a real distinction.

Here Duns Scotus and his followers make an appearance and suggest that we ought to recognize a formal distinction or non-identity whenever we can think abstractly about an element of fact in isolation from another with which it nevertheless makes up a concrete unity. A mind in the concrete is both intellect and will, and intellect and will are not distinct things; yet we are correct in saying that the intellect is not the will, for the meanings of these terms are formally distinct.[1] Hence a formal distinction is more than logical, for it reproduces the structure of fact, but it is less than a real distinction between concrete facts.

This suggestion is not without its attractions, for it simplifies the relation of thought to fact and asserts the closest possible correspondence between the structure of thought and the structure of fact. Yet it also arouses certain misgivings. However useful and necessary our analytic

[1] "Licet haec sit vera: Substantia intellectiva est volitiva, ubi est praedicatio concretiva unius perfectionis de altera, tamen haec negatur: Intellectus est voluntas, quia illa significant perfectiones illas ut abstractas a se invicem et secundum proprias formalitates" (Duns Scotus, *Opus Oxoniense*, I, d.5, q.1, no. 6).

dissection of fact may be in order that we should grasp the real adequately, dare we introduce into reality itself distinctions exactly corresponding with the partial aspects gradually revealed to our tentative and imperfect thinking? If we are thinking correctly, however imperfectly, the real must be such as to offer these aspects to the mind, but is that the same as saying that it contains a readymade distinction of formalities which we do nothing but discover? Does not one important kind of progress in thinking consist in grasping as one what we had previously been unable to bring together? Would not perfect thinking dispense altogether with our tentative and often clumsy attempts at analysis?

Moreover, if we admit a formal distinction with this measure of ontological validity, we seem condemned to follow infinite regresses in the analysis of reality itself. We could scarcely avoid acknowledging the distinguishable parts of the continuum, whether spatial or temporal, to be formally distinct in fact, but such parts are distinguishable *ad infinitum*. If we begin thinking of a relation as formally distinct from its terms, we inevitably tend to think of other relations between the terms and the primary relation, and so on again *ad infinitum*. We certainly appear to be turning the world into an unearthly ballet of bloodless categories.

These considerations may help us to return with greater sympathy to the more modest conception of a logical distinction with a foundation in fact and to explore what legitimate meaning might be given to this phrase. The discrimination of the real and the logical distinction may be examined with the aid of the one question which we have hitherto discussed in detail, that of essence and existence. The movement of the mind in making the affirmation of existence is a movement from conceptual assimilation to factual reference, the addition to *what* is of the fact *that* it is. But we found that we could not import this distinction into fact as it stands. When, to put it crudely, we started from the other end, from the fact of existence, we found that the notion of being overflowed into the modes of being; the distinction that we had finally to make was between being and its limitation by individual quiddity. That was a genuine opposition and tension in fact; that was a real distinction discovered by the mind and not made by it. By contrast our initial distinction of positive essence and the bare fact of existence was seen to be due to the functions of the human mind as receptive and projective, but it was not a purely verbal distinction; reality offered itself to us under those aspects. The distinction has a foundation in fact, but it was a logical distinction inasmuch as it applied to fact only in its relationship to mind.

It might perhaps be said that to speak in such cases of a formal distinction is to emphasize its foundation in fact, while to speak of a logical distinction is to stress its character as an aspect for thought, so that both expressions are legitimate. It would be pernickety to dispute so conciliatory a suggestion, but it is important to remember that, if people want to speak of a formal distinction, they should not regard it as pertaining to fact except in relation to mind; otherwise they will be turning fact into a bundle of abstractions. If we prefer to speak in Thomistic fashion of a logical distinction, this is because the term makes clear both that it is a distinction of aspects which fact presents to the analytic activity of mind and that, since it is a legitimate distinction of aspects, fact reveals itself therein as destined to mind and patient of the activities of thought. Consequently, in discriminating distinctions, we have to ask whether the addition of one factor to the other is an addition of reality or merely another aspect under which the same reality appears to a fuller understanding of it. In the former case the distinction is real; in the latter the distinction is logical but, unless we are merely replacing one verbal formula by another with the same meaning, it has a foundation in fact.

We must add that a real distinction as thus defined does

not of itself imply separability. There is a real distinction of being and quiddity, but it would be nonsensical to suppose that one could exist without the other. Even where such a supposition is not nonsensical, it is not necessarily possible in fact. If a valid synthetic entailment is conceivable, this means that really distinct existents may yet be inseparably associated; the importance of this point will become evident when we discuss cause and effect. Therefore, to answer the question whether one thing or element of fact could exist without another calls for more than a discussion whether they are really distinct in the sense here intended. But the sense in which we speak of a real distinction is important, for it pertains to the structure of fact as fact in contrast with the aspects which fact presents to thought, and it is the business of the metaphysician to try to penetrate to the structure of fact as fact.

3

Distinction implies relatedness, and otherness is the most elementary of relations. Like distinctions, the kinds of relation could be discriminated in innumerable ways. In Aristotle's scheme of categories the three absolute or non-relative categories, substance, quantity and quality, are followed by relation itself and then by six headings which may be regarded as kinds of relationship to which Aristotle attributed special importance. These are place, date, posture, possession, activity and passivity. Such, at any rate, is the list in the *Categories* and the *Topics*, but it does not recur elsewhere in the same form, nor does it seem to have any great moment for Aristotle's systematic philosophy. Hence the question why Aristotle selected precisely these kinds of relationship may be described as a puzzle, but one of no great interest.

From a logical point of view we distinguish symmetrical from non-symmetrical relations. If the subject of relation is called the referent and the term to which this is related is called the relatum, then a relation is symmetrical when the relatum must have the same relation to the referent. Thus, if A is equal to B, B is equal to A. But, if A is a brother of B, B may be either a brother or a sister of A; such a relation is simply non-symmetrical. In other cases the relatum cannot have the same relation to the referent; if A is greater than B, B cannot be greater than A. Such a relation can be described more definitely as asymmetrical.

A similar division is based on the property of transitivity. A relation is transitive when, if A is thus related to B and B similarly related to C, A must also have this relation to C. If A is an ancestor of B and B an ancestor of C, A must be an ancestor of C. But, if A is a friend of B and B is a friend of C, it does not follow that A is a friend of C; such a relation is non-transitive. An intransitive relation is one in which, when A is thus related to B and B thus related to C, A cannot be similarly related to C. For example, if A is twice as large as B and B twice as large as C, A cannot be twice as large as C.

Relations may also be classified, according to the number of instances which each term may have when the other is specified, as of many to many, of many to one, of one to many, and of one to one. Thus, if A is greater than B, there may be many other things which are greater than B and many others which are less than A; being greater and being less are many-many relations. Createdness is a many-one relation and creation a one-many relation, for there can be only one creator but many creatures. In a monogamous society at any given time husband and wife designate one-one relations.

Apart from dyadic relations between two terms there may be triadic and tetradic relations and, conceivably, polyadic relations involving any number of terms. Giving is a triadic relation involving a donor, a recipient and a gift. Jealousy is a triadic relation, for A is jealous of B on account of B's intimacy with C. Contemporary logic, stimulated by the work of Bertrand Russell, has made use of these principles of classification to develop an elegant calculus of relational arguments which is a quite genuine achievement. Some reference to it has been included here because it is necessary for clear thinking about relations, but, as it stands, it is a logical instrument. The metaphysician has to ask a more general question about the place of relations in the real world.

That relatedness is a feature of the real world is undeniable. The world does not consist of atomic facts to which thinking contributes the connections; the world is presented to us in experience as an interconnected manifold. Hence there can be no question about the reality of many forms of relatedness; the relations which we perceive to obtain between really distinct terms are real relations, being no less real than the terms between which they obtain.

On the other hand, where there is only a logical distinction, there can evidently be only a logical relation. For example, the classical definition of man as a rational animal is formally a piece of logical analysis; it does not entitle us to say that there is in man a real factor called animality and another called rationality. Hence the relation of animality to rationality in man is a logical relation of genus to specific difference; the relationship of body and soul is a different kind of distinction and has a different claim to reality. In general, the distinctions and relations which we set up when analysing in terms of essence are logical distinctions and relations; it is only when we are thinking in terms of being that we find real distinctions and real relations. If we say that there is a real distinction and a real relation of body and soul, this is because we hold that body and soul are principles of being and not merely isolable features in logical or essential analysis. The claim of any relation to be a real relation depends, therefore, on showing that it subsists or appears when our thinking becomes genuinely ontological.

Even when we have recognized a real relation, however, we are faced with the problem of where its reality resides. Has it a distinct reality of its own or does its reality coincide with that of its terms? The truth that some relations are real has led many Thomists to assert that they have a reality distinct from their foundation in the terms which they relate. One way, although it is scarcely a Thomistic way, of upholding this would be to think of a relation as a peculiar form of unity characterizing a manifold precisely in its diversity. In this view a relation would really coincide with its converse relation. That A is equal to B and B is equal to A, and that A is a parent of B and B is a child of A, are instances of logical equivalence; they would thus also be examples of a real identity of relation. It is by no means nonsensical to speak of a relation as a form of unity of a manifold in its diversity, but the diversity is then presupposed and subsists within the relatedness of the terms. Hence, if A and B are really distinct, we must admit that the relation of A to B really belongs to A and that the relation of B to A really belongs to B. Those who uphold the doctrine of a real distinction of relations from their foundation have usually, therefore, maintained it in the form that there is a real distinction between A and the relation of A to B, between B and the relation of B to A, and equally between the relation of A to B and the relation of B to A.

Bradley's argument for the unreality of relations can be taken as a criticism of this position.

The relation is not the adjective of one term, for, if so, it does not relate. Nor for the same reason is it the adjective of each term taken apart, for then again there is no relation between them. Nor is the relation their common property, for then what keeps them apart?[1]

---

[1] F. H. Bradley, *Appearance and Reality*, Oxford 1930, p. 27; cf. the whole argument of chs. i–ii.

When we have chopped up reality in this manner, we seem to need new relations to unite each term with its relation and to unite each relation with its converse, and so on *ad infinitum*. We need not conclude with Bradley that relations are unreal, but it does seem hard to suppose them to have a distinct reality of their own.

There is no doubt, of course, that logically, on the side of essence, what a thing is in itself is a distinct item, or set of items, from what it is in relation to other things. But, in order to assert or deny a real distinction, we must ask an ontological question; we must ask whether relations enhance the being or increase the reality of their terms. Suppose a body of a certain size to exist. Another body of the same size comes into existence. Between these bodies now subsists a relation of equality. The former body then ceases to exist, and the relation of equality ceases also. Can we really think that the being of the former was enhanced when its fellow came into existence and that the being of the latter was diminished when the former ceased to be? Anything but a negative answer to this question would be manifestly absurd.

What, then, is the fallacy at the bottom of the assertion that real relations have a distinct reality of their own? It is the gratuitous assumption that the world consists of atomic absolutes that entails the absurd conclusion that new elements of being are needed in order to relate these absolutes together. In reality the things of experience exhibit both absolute and relative aspects in the unity of their being, and the logical actualization of a relative aspect through the coming-to-be of the appropriate relatum is no enhancement of being to the referent; it is merely how the referent now presents itself to thought in its togetherness with the relatum.

While this is fairly obvious with relations such as equality, we might still ask whether it is true of all relations. Hume's classification of relations might suggest that it was not. For

Hume distinguishes "such as depend entirely on the ideas, which we compare together, and such as may be chang'd without any change in the ideas".[1] If some relations could be different without any difference in the terms, it would seem to follow that they are really distinct from the terms. In contrast with resemblance, proportion in quality or number, degrees in any quality, and contrariety, which Hume correctly regards as logically dependent on their terms, he asserts that identity, causation and relations of time and place are independent of their terms. Nor is the assertion unplausible, especially when we think of things as changing position without any other change in them.

Turning our minds to causation, however, or to originative relations in general, for causation both by Hume and since has been usually restricted to a temporal relation of antecedent and consequent, we wonder whether we are asking the right question when we ask whether they bring a new relation into existence. We can properly ask whether they are a source of new reality, and by their definition we must answer in the affirmative, but the new reality of which they are the source is the whole reality of what is originated and not a mere relation. Of relations in time we may say that there would be no temporal relations unless there were change and that there would be no change unless there were causation. Hence the reality of relations in time appears to be reducible to causal relations when adequately considered. Identity as understood by Hume is the identity of a person or thing throughout its history and so should, in Hume's context, be reducible to a peculiar sort of temporal and causal relation. If, unlike Hume, we believe in a simple persistence of substance, identity ceases to be a relation at all.

Spatial relations remain as the one field in which it seems difficult to deny that the relation is something different from the terms. In the abstract, movement can be described as a simple change of spatial relations and of nothing else. If

[1] Hume, *Treatise of Human Nature*, ed. Selby-Bigge, bk. i, pt. 3, s. i, p. 69.

I am thinking only of spatial relations, there is no difference between saying that I travel to Edinburgh and saying that Edinburgh comes to me. But, in the concrete, there is an immense difference. If I want to be in Edinburgh, it is useless to beckon to the capital of Scotland to come to me; I have to buy a ticket and board a train and make the journey. That is to say, I have to go through certain causal processes, and on the commonsense level we describe that thing as moving which is in causal process and that as static which is not. There is no difficulty, then, in seeing that change of spatial relation finds its reality in causation.

What, however, must we say of an existent spatial relation? Because we are inclined to confuse real three-dimensional space with the two-dimensional extension of the visual datum, so we are inclined to suppose that the simple relations of contiguity of coloured expanses are reproduced in the relations of real space. I should venture to suggest that the axioms of Euclidean geometry are intuitively certain in their application to visual extension, but that does not justify their application to real space, and contemporary physical investigation tends to show that they do not thus apply exactly. So the visual datum is a single real whole, and to pick out its parts is an analytic mental process, but this need not be the case with real space. In fact, when we reflect on our experience of being corporeal and of being in contact with other bodies, we find that the occupation of real space, or more precisely the maintenance of volume, is a matter of dynamic relations with other bodies. Real spatial relations have a reciprocal causal character. In general, then, all relations which are a source of new reality can be reduced, as we might have expected, to the originative type of relation.

Thus it seems that there are three questions which we can ask about the reality of relations and to which the answers are as follows. Are there real relations? Yes, relatedness is as much a feature of the real world as terms in relation;

the world is presented to us as an interconnected whole from which terms and their relations have to be analytically distinguished. Are relations ever the source of new reality? Yes, that is precisely the nature of the originative type of relation and, wherever we find a relation which gives rise to novelty, we should look for the originative relation or relations involved in it. Are the relations which we discover in the world of experience ever really distinct from the terms which they relate? No, for to say so would be to convert relations into pseudo-absolutes; they are logically distinct aspects of things in their togetherness. [1]

[1] Cf. the excellent brief discussion of relations in L. de Raeymaeker: *La Philosophie de l'Etre*, Louvain, 1947, pp. 234-6, in which the essentially relative character of finite being is shown to forbid the attribution of distinct reality to relations. "La raison substantielle de la limitation est en même temps la raison substantielle de la relativité."

CHAPTER V

Similarity and Analogy

I

I F THE relation of similarity deserves separate treatment, this is because it is the ontological way of describing what on the epistemological side is the question of universals. The fact, to put it at its lowest and least controversial level, that we employ class-terms and attribute the same predicate to many subjects, as when Fido, Ponto and Rover are all called dogs, gives rise to one of the most venerable of philosophical problems. Moreover it has sometimes been thought to have the most far-reaching metaphysical consequences. However this may be, it certainly has some metaphysical consequences. Variations in the kind of foundation in fact which we suppose the use of universal terms to have are variations in the way in which we conceive the metaphysical structure of reality.

The traditional classification of opinions on the problem of universals is not altogether satisfying. We are told that there are nominalists for whom the sole community in the members of a class is one of name. Conceptualists are said to find this community solely in a mental operation. Moderate realists admit the necessity of the mental activity of abstraction for the formation of universal concepts but provide this activity with a justification in the structure of fact. Extreme realists are said to hold that distinctions in fact correspond exactly with the distinctions of abstract thought.

For the nominalist as thus defined, classification is completely arbitrary. There is no more reason why we should select Fido, Ponto and Rover to be classified as dogs than any other collection of objects, such as the moon, logic and muchness. Has anyone ever really held such a doctrine? Philosophers have not been guiltless of absurdities, but these have usually been comparatively subtle absurdities; we look in vain through the history of philosophy for anyone who has been guilty of so crude an absurdity as that which we have just described. Philosophers who have called themselves or who have been called nominalists have certainly insisted that the problem of universals is primarily a question of language, but they have not denied anything so obvious as that significant classification presupposes a similarity of quality or of relationship.

About conceptualism much the same remark has to be made. The mental activity postulated is not simply arbitrary; it is a selection of relevant similarities. Where the conceptualist differs from the nominalist is in the acknowledgment of a specific mental process as a preliminary to the use of a common term, but a real similarity is equally presupposed. Hence there does not seem to be much to separate the conceptualist from the moderate realist who recognizes that abstraction has a justification in fact, for this justification is obviously the fact of similarity.

An extreme realist would, no doubt, have a point of view of his own. If distinctions of fact corresponded exactly with abstractions, the world would be a system of universals and individuality would be no more than deceptive appearance. It is true that Hegelians have gone so far as to describe the world of individual persons and things as a world of appearance, but even for them that appearance is not a deceptive appearance but a necessary stage in the mind's penetration into reality. As with nominalism, so with extreme realism, we must ask whether any philosopher has upheld the doctrine without mitigation or modification. Yet there has been much dispute about universals. Let us see what philosophers have really said about them and wherein the genuine differences lie.

2

The first point to notice about the Platonic doctrine of Forms is that it is not really an explanation of the predication of universal terms at all. If the use of such terms implies that there are eternal exemplars in which the things of experience participate in their degree, then a sentence such as "John is a man" means "John approximates to, or participates in, the universal Form of man". Instead of having to explain how many subjects can all be said to be men, we have now the exactly parallel task of explaining how they can all be said to participate in the Form of man. The sense in which this can be upheld remains undecided. Hence Plato can hardly be classified as an extreme realist about universals; what he has done is to postulate a new type of singular, the Forms.

If this theory can be justified, of course, it is certainly an assertion that universal predication has metaphysical consequences. This assertion turns out, however, to belong not to general metaphysics but to natural theology. For the Neoplatonists were plainly right to think of the Forms as an intelligible system and to unite them in the hypostasis of the *Nous*, and St. Thomas's acknowledgment of the Forms as the divine creative ideas provides them with an unambiguous place in fact within the context of a theistic philosophy. Hence the metaphysical basis of the doctrine of the Forms lies outside our present subject.

Aristotle brings the Forms down to earth by making them intrinsic to the members of the class which they specify. In reality universals are inseparable from the individuality of individual things, but they are isolated by the abstractive activity of intellect. Humanity really exists in John, but it is not really distinct from what constitutes John as John; it only comes to be a distinct object for thought. It would seem that a consistent Aristotelian theory should begin with singulars and should ask what is meant by resemblance among singulars and how we come to recognize resemblances.

In fact, however, Aristotle remains half a Platonist by continuing to approach the problem from the other direction. It is the universal that he takes for granted; his problems are, metaphysically, how the universal form can be individuated and, logically, how we can come to know the singular. Aristotle has been variously classified by a conceptualist or a moderate realist, but there is much to be said for describing him, if not as an extreme, at least as a somewhat immoderate realist. This note is reproduced in thirteenth-century Aristotelianism, and Duns Scotus's doctrine of distinct formalities corresponding with the distinctions of universal concepts can scarcely be said to be more than a sharpening of the realism inherent in Aristotle himself.

William of Ockham reacted directly against this Scotist theory, and, whatever may be said against some of the tendencies of Ockham's logic, it does seem that he deserves the credit of having transcended the residue of Platonism and made an independent empirical approach to the problem of universals. We are primarily aware of singulars, and the recognition of the similarities among singulars upon which classification is based is a gradual process and usually no more than an approximate achievement. Metaphysics might quite well have been critically reconstructed on this foundation, but the unfortunate tendency of the followers of Ockham was to suppose that we never attained concepts of a sufficient degree of clearness to furnish evident principles of thought and being. This was a gratuitous exaggeration intelligible only as an historical reaction against the Scotist opposite extreme.

In modern philosophy Hobbes states roundly that there is "nothing in the world universal but names; for the things named are every one of them individual and singular".[1] Hence, just as Odo of Tournai in the eleventh century, who went to the length of saying that there was a single human nature of which individual men were distinct properties, may be set down as a genuine extreme realist, so Hobbes

[1] Hobbes, *Leviathan*, pt. i, ch. iv.

76

may perhaps be regarded as the one genuine nominalist in the history of philosophy. But it may be doing too much honour both to Odo and to Hobbes to suppose that they had really thought out what they were saying. For, in the case of Hobbes, it is too clear that it is impossible to ask whether there are real similarities without answering affirmatively, and, even if the nominalist position is assumed, the same difficulty recurs about words as about things. For the word "man" is a class of noises or of marks on paper, and we can speak of the same word only because we detect the similarity whether of the noises or of the marks. Nominalism, as literally understood, solves nothing at all, and obviously solves nothing at all.

Locke is quite clear that everything real is individual, but that there are real similarities in nature. What confuses him is that he supposes that there must be a special kind of mental object to serve as a universal idea. Consequently he tries to suggest how some particular ideas may somehow come to stand for others:

. . . which is done by considering them as they are in the mind such appearances separate from all other existences, and the circumstances of real existence, as time, place, or any other concomitant ideas. . . . Such precise, naked appearances in the mind, without considering how, whence, or with what others they came there, the understanding lays up (with names commonly annexed to them) as the standards to rank real existences into sorts, as they agree with these patterns, and to denominate them accordingly. Thus, the same colour being observed today in chalk or snow, which the mind yesterday received from milk, it considers that appearance alone, makes it a representative of all of that kind, and, having given it the name "whiteness", it by that sound signifies the same quality wheresoever to be imagined or met with; and thus universals, whether ideas or terms, are made.[1]

[1] Locke, *Essay Concerning Human Understanding*, bk. ii, ch. xi, §9.

The objection to this is that the colours of chalk, snow and milk, however similar, remain distinct particulars, and there is as much difficulty about one standing for the others as there is about eating chalk instead of cheese. When Berkeley denies universal ideas in this sense but asserts the power of mind to attend exclusively to the points in which things are similar, he is really putting forward the doctrine of universal thinking in the only sense in which it is intelligible. For, while he attacks Locke's theory of abstract ideas, he adds in the second edition of the *Principles* that "it must be acknowledged that a man may consider a figure merely as triangular, without attending to the particular qualities of the angles, or relations of the sides".[1] Here he shows the customary good sense which persists even when he is at his most paradoxical.

Hume congratulates Berkeley for his denial of abstract ideas but proceeds to put forward a doctrine which is much more like that of Locke.[2] The reason is obvious. He cannot, like Berkeley, admit a power of intellectual discrimination without accepting a view of mental activity which is quite foreign to his philosophy; he has, therefore, to make particular ideas somehow stand for other particular ideas. His only difference from Locke is that he frankly admits that they continue to be particular while having a tendency to call up other related particulars. Thus, on the question of universals, Berkeley stands on one side and Locke and Hume stand together on the other, Berkeley acknowledging a kind of intellectual activity which the others deny.

3

These historical glimpses suggest that there are real divisions of opinion on the question of universals but that these are not quite so sharply defined as is sometimes supposed. Since our business is with the ontological order,

[1] Berkeley, *Principles of Human Knowledge*, Intro., §16.
[2] Hume, *Treatise of Human Nature*, bk. i, pt. i, s. 7.

we must relate these differences to the meaning of similarity. The nominalist can hardly be supposed to deny the occurrence of real similarities, but he prefers not to have to discuss what similarity implies. The one plain and indubitable fact for him is that we use the same name to designate all the members of a class. But the nominalist must realize when he reflects that he is faced with the same problem about the classes of similar noises or of similar marks which we describe as the same word. He cannot escape discussing the similarity of words and may just as well consent to discuss the similarity of things.

Now similarity may be roughly explained as partial identity and partial diversity. The kind and degree of identity which it involves is the justification of a measure of realism about universals, but any exaggeration of this identity will give rise to an excessive realism. The view that there was something really distinct and identical in each of two similar things would evidently fall under this condemnation. For the partial identity and partial diversity in which similarity consists are not the identity of a part and the diversity of another part. Two chairs have no *thing* in common although they cannot be said to have nothing in common. The appearance of paradox here is purely verbal, for in ordinary usage to have something in common simply means to be alike and does not imply the common possession of anything concrete.

The relative obviousness of the position that two chairs or two trees or two men are wholly different in the concrete, and that concrete reality is necessarily individual, has tended to restrain philosophers from denying it too blatantly. Any step towards denying it is a step towards turning reality into a system of universals. But, as we have noticed, some philosophers have been inclined to suppose that the activity of abstraction resulted in the formation of at least a special kind of intellectual object which could be set before the mind and contemplated as a self-contained unity. This is how an exaggerated realism seems genuinely to make an appearance in the history of philosophy. For, if abstraction were a neat dissection of this kind, it would be difficult to uphold its validity without acknowledging something very like a real distinction between the universal aspects and the individuality of things. The Scotist formal distinction in its full rigour seems at least to be required. It is not certain that we could logically stop even there and refrain from regarding individual things as appearance and reality as a system of universals.

Reflection, however, does not bear out this theory. When I think of this man as a man or of this blue surface as blue, I am not conscious of any new object before me. I am only considering the same object in a different way; my awareness is differentiated and concentrated on a certain aspect of the object but the object itself remains the same. Here Ockham is in the right against Scotus, and Berkeley in the right against Locke. From this point of view the ambiguous nature of conceptualism can be judged. If it be taken to mean that universal thinking involves the formation of a special kind of object, it is false; if it means that universal thinking is a specific differentiation of awareness, it is true.

The whole matter can be summed up on the ontological level by trying to say more precisely what we mean by similarity. When we say that things are similar if they are partly identical and partly diverse, we do not mean that there is a part which is identical and parts which are diverse; the things as wholes manifest both identity and diversity to thought. Hence, while the notion of similarity may be said to be halfway between complete identity and utter diversity, and is therefore intelligible by its relationship to identity and diversity, it is a distinctive notion in its own right which is not strictly reducible to a combination of identity and diversity. Similarity is intrinsically an ultimate to be understood on its own account although with relation to identity and diversity.

Hence the awareness of similarity is a specific mental

activity in which a single act of thinking is a partial awareness of a plurality of objects. If some contemporary philosophers demand evidence that thinking is a specific activity, they may well be asked to find it in the function of comparison. For, if they try to reduce this to the imposition of a common name, they are left with precisely the same kind of problem about how we recognize the similarity of noises and of marks on paper; if they want to attribute the whole character of the process to the object as it is in the concrete, they will have to turn reality into a system of universals.

We have still to advert to the notion of exact similarity. When we say that two things are blue, we are attributing to them the possession of any of a set of visual qualities within a certain range. They may be light blue or dark blue; they may be a greenish blue or may approximate towards the violet end of the scale. But there is no appearance which is simply blue and nothing else; blue is essentially the name of a variable. On the other hand, we may assert or conjecture that two things are of exactly the same shade of blue. Here we have a determinate appearance which is this shade of blue, and it is here that we might be tempted to assert a real identity of being and not only an abstract identity to thought. But two visual data, even if they are of exactly the same shade of blue, remain diverse things. We must, therefore, admit a notion of exact similarity which does not involve real identity. Exact similarity consists in the common possession of a fully determinate quality within a certain field of determination, but that quality is still an abstraction from the concrete wholeness of the things which possess it. The distinction between approximate and exact similarity, however, brings us to the distinction between the analogous and the univocal.

4

Once again it was a theological stimulus which aroused the attention of philosophers to the importance of analogy. We want to be able to say something about God beyond simply that absolute being exists, but all our notions are derived from finite things. It is evident that any fully determinate notion derived from finite things will apply only to a specific class of finite things and to nothing else. We can utter true statements about absolute being only if we can liberate some of our notions from their finite determinacy. To say that the absolute manifests a determinate shade of blue would be an excessive absurdity; any determinate shade of blue excludes infinitely more than it asserts. Even blue in its vaguest and most indeterminate sense is essentially a characteristic of finite surfaces and, consequently, a notion which implies limitation. Hence the problem of finding anything to say validly of absolute being is the problem of finding notions which do not essentially imply limitation. Since the notion of being itself is most centrally of this kind, the attention of theistic philosophers has been devoted mainly to the universal applicability or analogy of the notion of being, but they have made an effort to exhibit this within the context of a general theory of analogy.

The classical scholastic doctrine of analogy is to be found in the work of Cajetan, *De Nominum Analogia.* It is worth noting that this professes to deal primarily with the analogy of names or words, for the first kind of analogy recognized by Cajetan, the analogy of attribution, is essentially linguistic. Health is in its central meaning a characteristic of living things, but food can be called healthy in so far as it ministers to health and a complexion can be called healthy in so far as it manifests health, and so forth. The analogy of attribution between these various meanings of healthy is simply a matter of the use of the same verbal symbol with different but related meanings; it has nothing to do with metaphysics.

Metaphysical significance is attributed by Cajetan to the analogy of proportionality. Here again we must first eliminate the analogy of improper proportionality which belongs to figures of speech; this kind of use of terms involves not only the finding of a similarity but the association of a dissimilarity in order to give concrete vividness to the similarity. The lion is called the king of beasts because his relationship to other animals is like that of a king to his subjects, but the full associations of human kingship, although inappropriate to animals, are invoked in order to give life to the comparison. We are here in the realm of metaphor.

When metaphor is excluded, we have the analogy of proper proportionality; this is chiefly exemplified in the divine attributes. If we say that God is good, we mean something, but we are certainly not attributing to God the same limited perspectives and laborious efforts that are characteristic of human virtue. At least we are saying that the divine goodness is to the divine being as human goodness is to human nature. Here is an identity or similarity of proportion, however different the terms involved may be.

That this may be described in the manner of literary criticism as suggestive we shall not deny, but it is hardly satisfying on the level of philosophical precision. In the first place, is this an identity or a similarity of proportion? More accurately, in the terms that we have put forward as appropriate to the concrete, is it an exact or an approximate similarity? Presumably it is an approximate similarity, since we are not in a field in which we can apply the mathematical exactness of $a: b = c: d$.

More seriously, does this really help us to know anything about the nature of divine goodness if we know nothing else about it? For the divine being in general transcends our knowledge in precisely the same way. To say that human goodness is to human nature as divine goodness is to the being of God seems to be no more than to say that human goodness is to human nature as x is to y. The latter side of the equation consists of two unknowns. It does not seem that we are being enlightened at all unless, more simply and more fundamentally, there is some similarity between divine and finite being and between divine and finite goodness in spite of all the difference. There can be no doubt that such a fundamental similarity is presupposed if we are going to be able to say anything significant about absolute being at all.

The question of analogy is, then, an extension of the question of similarity, and we want to say that, if we approach the question on its widest front and without special theological reference, it has ramifications throughout our thinking. For only the similarity of the exactly similar, of a fully determinate quality within a certain range of determination, deserves the name of univocal. The blueness of a fully determinate shade of blue is univocal and unambiguous, but blueness in general cannot be separated from its possible shades and may be verified in a multitude of different ways. It should be described as an analogous term.

Once again, then, we are faced with the contrast between notions which are open and indeterminate and notions which are closed and determinate. Moreover a notion may be closed in one respect and open in another. Blueness is open in so far as it may be verified in any and every shade of blue, but it is closed and determinate in so far as it is applicable only to visual surfaces. There are, therefore, degrees of the character of analogy between the fully determinate and notions which can be verified in different ways over the whole range of being. The classical emphasis on the analogy of being is justified to the extent that being is the altogether and utterly analogous term, and the analogy of being has its special importance in regard to theological affirmation.

At present, however, we are dealing with general metaphyics. On this plane our meditations on the relation of similarity may not have yielded any imposing positive results, but they may have had an effect in dissipating some of the philosophical fog which tends to obscure the problems of universal concepts and of analogy. And the notion of similarity is at least of some interest for its own sake in the unanalysable way in which it mediates between identity and diversity.

CHAPTER VI

Unity, Diversity and Number

I

THE RELATION of similarity is the foundation of number. For things can be enumerated in so far as they manifest a similarity either of intrinsic quality or of relation. There are five chairs in my study, for there are five distinct objects which are similar in respect of being chairs in my study. A difficulty might be suggested if there were also a soapbox which I used as a chair in an emergency. Are there then five chairs or six? The difficulty, however, is merely about the definition of "chair". According to the precise definition chosen for the word it would be a fact either that there were five chairs or that there were six.

A pure similarity of relationship is, of course, sufficient for enumeration. If during the last five minutes I have been thinking of metaphysics, my friend's illness and the grocer's bill, these can be enumerated as three objects of my thought during that period although they have nothing else in common. Any number, therefore, is a notion of second order, being a similarity of classes defined by a similarity of first order. Hence the well-known Russellian definition of a number in extensional terms as a class of classes in which the members of each stand to the members of the others in a one-one relation. Number in general is a third-order notion, since to be a number means belonging to the series constituted by such classes of classes.

It should be stated explicitly that enumeration presupposes not only a similarity of different objects but a similarity of

85

different and mutually exclusive objects. I can legitimately ask how many chairs there are in the room, but it would be nonsensical to ask how many things there are in the room. For a chair is a thing, and likewise the seat or the leg of a chair is a thing, and no addition is possible between a thing and its parts. Similarly non-enumerable characters are unity and wholeness, for the parts of a complex unity are unities of a different kind and the parts of a complex whole are wholes of a different kind. In other cases the difficulty could be overcome by more precise definition. In a list of educational establishments at Oxford is the university to count as one or the colleges as many? This is a matter of definitory choice; the only choice which is logically impossible would be to add up the university with the colleges. The point involved in all this is akin to the difficulty which led Russell to state that, in spite of first appearances, no class could be a member of itself, and it possesses a similar interest in being a case where an apparently intelligible form of words turns out to be literally meaningless.

The metaphysical question about numbers, however, concerns their status in reality. Since the mathematical sciences are the most obvious fields of demonstrative inference, the opponents of metaphysics have been very much concerned to show that they give us no information about the real world. For, if they did give us such information, it would seem to follow that there must be true synthetic *a priori* propositions to serve as premisses for fruitful inference. Yet this is by no means evident, for the fact that arithmetical and algebraical reasoning consists largely in the transformation of sets of symbols into other symbols with which they are equal lends colour to the view that these processes of thought are purely analytic or tautological.

Nevertheless the rules for the transformation of arithmetical and algebraical symbols do not appear to be either arbitrary or tautological. No doubt any symbols other than those in use might have been chosen to carry their meaning, and the symbols actually in use might have been given a different meaning, but, when their meaning has once been decided, the rules for their transformation depend upon their meaning and cannot be other than they are. It would be futile to protest to one's bank manager that in one's private symbolism red ink signifies a credit. Moreover, although the rules of transformation are usually taken for granted in writing out a calculation, they are the genuine major premises of the argument; they are not merely presuppositions like the principle of contradiction. And they are synthetic propositions in the Kantian sense; that $4 \times 9 = 36$ follows from, but is not contained in, the definitions of 4, 9, 36 and the operation of multiplying.

In geometrical argument, since the premises are usually expressed in full and we are dealing directly with geometrical notions and not with the transformation of symbols, it is clear enough that we are engaged in a deductive process and one which is not merely analytic. The trouble here is with the status of the first principles or axioms, especially the parallel axiom. While there is so much difference of opinion among mathematicians on the question, it would be foolish for a philosopher to attempt to settle it. Hence we must leave in abeyance the problem of the relation of geometrical reasoning to the real world.

Nevertheless our business is with numbers, and we can assert their relevance to the real world without hesitation. Numerical properties belong to relational situations. Duality belongs to a situation in which there is A_1 distinct from A_2 but resembling A_2 in being A, threeness to a situation in which there is A_1 distinct from A_2 and A_3 but resembling them in being A, and so forth. It is far more troublesome to set out the situation in words than to understand what it is. But there are real distinctions and real relations of similarity between distinct things; hence there are real numerical properties. In the same way the relationships between numbers really apply to the instances of these numbers.

If, of course, we ask whether numerical properties are a source of new reality or are really distinct from the groups to which they belong, the answer is obviously negative. They are only logically distinct aspects of the groups to which they belong. That, presumably, is the reason why they have so easily been dismissed as mere creations of thinking or of symbolism. But that is just as unreasonable an extreme as to think of numerical properties as independent entities. Hence the advantage of a terminology which enables us to speak of numbers as real while admitting that they are only logically distinct from the concrete wholes of which they are aspects.

2

Numerical plurality, and consequently also numerical unity, presupposes a similarity of the diverse. Diversity itself, to which is opposed the unity which is traditionally called transcendental, is more fundamental. Transcendental unity is so called because it belongs to absolutely everything and every collection of things; it is simply the self-identity by which, in Bishop Butler's famous phrase, "everything is what it is and not another thing". About the fundamental diversity opposed to it we may ask whether it entails dissimilarity. In other words, could there be two things which were exactly similar in all respects, so that they differed only by this being this and that being that? The negative answer to this question is the principle which, since the time of Leibniz, has been discussed under the name of the identity of indiscernibles and which McTaggart called the dissimilarity of the diverse.

Leibniz's system of monads shows how profoundly impressed he was by the uniqueness of each individual existent. Already in the *Discours de Métaphysique* addressed to Arnauld (1686) he denies that two substances can differ *solo numero*. He holds that St. Thomas's opinion that every purely spiritual being constitutes its own species should be applied to all substances, "pourvu qu'on prenne la différence spécifique comme la prennent les géomètres à l'égard de leurs figures".[1] The condition is not altogether clear, but it may be supposed that he wants every difference of character to be taken into account and not only such as a scholastic would commonly judge to indicate a difference of substantial nature.

In a letter to de Volder of 20th June 1703 Leibniz puts his principle in the form that things which differ must differ by somewhat or possess some recognizable diversity, calls this a most evident axiom, and wonders that it should not be universally received: "Quae differunt debent aliquo differre seu in se assignabilem habere diversitatem, mirumque est manifestissimum hoc axioma cum tot aliis ab hominibus adhibitum non fuisse." In the *Fifth Letter to Clarke*, however, where he spreads himself to a greater extent on the identity of indiscernibles, he does not profess to find the existence of indiscernibles intrinsically contradictory. He maintains his principle on the ground that the Creator could have no motive for producing two ·exactly similar things and assigning different histories to them; this would be contrary to the principle of sufficient reason. We should look at Clarke's own previous letter to see why Leibniz takes this line.

Clarke had maintained that two instances of "simple solid matter" of equal figure and dimensions were exactly alike and yet remained two, and that even with compound bodies there was no reason why two drops of water should not be exactly alike and yet be two. In his answer Leibniz has no recourse to relational properties, and without reference to relations it would scarcely seem plausible to deny the absolute possibility of exactly similar particles of matter. Hence, while he refrains from opposing the absolute possibility of such exact similars, he wants to maintain, first, that any proposed instances of exact similarity are merely the

---

[1] Leibniz, *Discours de Métaphysique*, §9.

abstractions of the physicist and do not correspond with concrete fact in its wholeness and, secondly, that concrete fact must consist of monads each mirroring the universe in a different way. This supposition alone, according to him, does justice to the principle of sufficient reason and is therefore worthy of creative wisdom.

Leibniz's position is not, then, altogether unambiguous. One retains a suspicion that he would have liked to accuse of contradiction the assertion of a multiplicity of indiscernibles. Yet, in face of opposition, he takes up a less intransigent attitude and declares this assertion to be incompatible only with the wisdom of the Creator. But, since he does not take relational properties into consideration, his discussion remains incomplete.

On the commonsense level it seems at first quite natural to suppose that, for example, two atoms of hydrogen are exactly similar in all respects and differ only in this being this and that being that. Yet this involves reducing individuality, thisness or thatness, to an arbitrary label attached to a set of characters and marking them off as an individual thing. Surely there are conditions of individuality which make it intelligible that this should be this and that should be that. When we try to speak of two things which possess the same quiddity limiting the same degree of being, we do not appear to escape contradiction. For in what do they differ?

At this point we are evidently impelled to ask whether a sufficient difference may not be found in relational properties. But not any kind of relation will do. A purely logical relation is useless, for we are concerned with an ontological distinction. It is useless to suggest that, with every distinct A and B, A has the exclusive property of being identical with A and B has the exclusive property of being identical with B. The logical relation of identity is ontologically no more than an absence of distinction and, consequently, an absence of relation. In any case such a suggestion begs the question, for the question is whether there can be A and B distinct but exactly similar in intrinsic character.

Nor would it suffice to invoke what we have called a real relation, since it is a real connection between really distinct terms, if it were not a source of new being. For once again we should be begging the question by presupposing that there could be two exactly similar things to enter into such a relation. The case, however, is different with the originative type of relation, in which one term is the source of the being of the other, or of part of the being of the other taken in its full concreteness. Here the consequent term does not exist independently of its relation to the antecedent term; in its coming into existence it differs from its antecedent precisely in being consequent upon it. Therefore, if the validity of the originative type of relation can be upheld, it supplies a type of relational property which will serve to distinguish things otherwise exactly similar.

In so far, then, as temporal relations can be analysed in terms of causal relations, and in so far as real spatial relations imply the limits of volume resulting from the dynamic contact of masses, temporal and spatial relations can be the source of individual differentiation. It is not contradictory to think of intrinsically exactly similar particles of matter which are yet different because they are, directly or indirectly, in a dynamic mutual spatial relation and of other exactly similar things coming to be in the course of time as the result of causal activity. Until we have discussed causation the real application of these notions remains doubtful, but what we have said suffices to show that the principle of the identity of indiscernibles does not entail the denial of the common-sense assumption that there are intrinsically exactly similar particles of matter.

Thus we can look at the principle without prejudice and ask whether it is really evident. I answer that it is evident, for, if things are exactly similar in all respects, how can they be distinct? It is not enough to retort that individuality is an irreducible factor, for it is one thing to say that a factor is irreducible and another to say that it can be arbitrarily applied. To assert that this and that can differ merely by being this and that is to make individuality into a character of being like any other character of being, and that is precisely to abolish individuality. It is the irreducibility of individuality which demands that it shall arise from a unique sum of being, and every individual quiddity must circumscribe a sum of being which is unique either in its intrinsic character or in its originative relations. Things may be exactly similar in one respect or another, but they cannot be exactly similar in all respects, for that would be to say that they were both the same and different, which is a manifest contradiction.

3

At this stage we might well gather together and supplement what we have said about individuality. The notion of individuality, of being this or that, is distinctive and irreducible to anything else. Everything that exists is individual; that is, individuality is, in the traditional phrase, a transcendental property of being. But individuality reveals two inseparable aspects, the unity or self-identity of the thing in itself and its distinction from anything else. Hence the scholastics in their list of the transcendental properties of being, after *ens* and *res* distinguished as the existent as such and the thing that exists, put *unum* and *aliquid*. *Unum* here signifies the unity of a thing in itself while *aliquid* is *aliud quid*, the thing in its distinction from everything else. With the remaining two transcendentals, *bonum* and *verum*, we are not yet concerned.

The world of experience falls into all kinds of overlapping unities with every sort and degree of unity in themselves and every sort and degree of distinction from what lies outside them. We have not yet discussed the notion of substance, which is based on a unity of activity and serves to differentiate the most important kind of real unity in the world. We shall not anticipate this discussion but, at the stage that we have reached, simply note the presence of unities in a more general and variable sense. The fullest unity seems to belong to two ends of the scale, to the most elementary particles of matter, whatever they may be, and to the most completely developed and integrated minds. In between comes the comparatively close unity of atoms and chemical compounds and living organisms. But there are many other looser kinds of real unity, like the unity of a forest or a river, of a family or a nation, and a teleological unity founded on human purpose belongs to tables, chairs, ploughs, swords. locomotives, aeroplanes and so forth.

Whatever thing or collection of things we are considering at the moment under the aspect of whatever unity belongs to it, it is always unique in its full concreteness. It is always being under a certain limitation or set of limitations which is individual. Being is the principle of similarity, of analogy, of participation; quiddity is the principle of dissimilarity, of finite determination, of individuality. In all finite things and in the finite world as a whole there are always present together in metaphysical composition and tension the aspects of similarity and of dissimilarity, of analogy and of determination, of participation and of individuality.

4

At this stage also, before we pass on to the second half of our inquiry and take explicit note of the factor of change, we might reflect on the nature of metaphysical thinking. It would be a mistake to say that ancient and medieval metaphysics were not critical, for philosophy has always been a criticism of thought and its presuppositions as well as an attempt at synthesis. But the more systematic modern criticism of knowledge compels the contemporary metaphysician to be more systematically critical in his approach.

We tried to sketch some of the chief difficulties at the beginning. A radical empiricism, like that of Hume, in which the rôle of thought is entirely overlooked, cannot lead to a metaphysic. The function of mind is reduced to a mere reception of impressions and reproduction of them in ideas, and it becomes mere verbiage to say that anything is or to ask what being implies. In so far as Hume's influence is still powerful in British philosophy, the way to a metaphysic remains closed. Anything other than having sensations and images has to be reduced to the construction or rather, on Humian assumptions, the spontaneous generation of symbolic systems, languages in the ordinary sense or languages like those of mathematical or logical symbolism.

It should really be sufficiently evident that such languages are not spontaneously generated but are the result of the constructive activity of mind. It is even more fundamentally evident that we not only have sensations but are aware of them and, through them, of ourselves and the external objects with which we are in interaction. Awareness can be differentiated without change in its objects, as when we perceive similarities and think in universal terms.

Recognition of the activity of thinking does not yet remove all obstacles to metaphysics. For we may, like Kant, take an ambiguous view of the validity of this activity and adopt the opinion that, while it is essential to the presentation of objects, it can only lead us to objects as they appear and never as they really are in themselves. Even if we take the most realistic interpretation of Kant's phenomenalism, our knowledge of things can never be more than a problematic approximation to what they really are. While we must obviously admit the highly limited character of human knowledge, there can be no metaphysic unless we know some things as they really are.

But how can we know things as they really are if we are not creative but receptive minds and can know things only by projecting what we receive from them? The answer is not only that we know ourselves to exist but that it is the basic character of knowing to be aware of being. If reflection informs us without doubt that we are aware that the world is, the fact of it is beyond question although the manner of it presents a set of problems to the epistemologist. Reflection on being and on the awareness of being in the existential judgment is not only the beginning of metaphysics but the foundation of a realistic theory of knowledge.

Nevertheless a critical metaphysic has to discriminate between what is due to the manner in which human knowledge is acquired and built up and what is inherent in the structure of fact itself. We must not logicize reality. Yet we must begin with our thinking in its concreteness and, since metaphysical insight is dependent on the activity of thought, must take logic fully into account. It would be unreasonable to complain that doing metaphysics involves doing much of logic all over again, for no other starting-point is available. To attempt to by-pass logic would be either to give free rein to the imagination or to fall into the trap of logicizing reality without knowing it.

Metaphysics, however, uses logic in order to transcend it. Not that we can reach a new type of thinking to which logic does not apply, but rather within and through the logical structure of thinking we attempt to discriminate and perceive the ontological structure of fact. The task is not like solving puzzles on the logical level which, once solved, can be dismissed, but seeks a glimpse of the permanent ontological significance of what appears on the logical level as a puzzle but can only be overcome by going beyond the merely logical level and examining it in terms of being.

Thus, beginning with the purely logical meaning of essence as subject and existence as predicate, we found that we could not make the matter fully intelligible without transforming it into an ontological tension of being and individual limitation. The distinctions made, and the relations set up, in the course of our thinking, had to be correspondingly discriminated in accordance with whether they represented genuine othernesses and genuine connections of being or were merely the result of the gradual and piecemeal development of human thought. In the same way we had to ask what thinking in universal terms really entailed in the things about which we think and what were the ontological conditions under which this is this and that is that.

Systematic metaphysics is not a universal pursuit, but all our thinking, as Kant recognized in his own way, involves a combination of empirical and metaphysical factors. The empirical factors are presented to the receptivity of mind; they are clear and unmistakable in their concreteness but offer varying types and degrees of difficulty to the effort to make them intelligible. The metaphysical factors appear in the course of mental activity; they can become clear in abstraction but their concrete application is often dubious and obscure. Neither can be isolated completely from the others, but their full harmony remains an ideal to which to approximate. In the attempt to build a critical metaphysic we look back to Aristotle for a structural design which has not been superseded and to Aquinas for an epistemological and ontological foundation in the awareness of being, and we accept from more recent philosophy the stimulus to a more consistent and systematic critical approach than was possible before the problems of knowledge received the amount of attention that they have received in modern times.

CHAPTER VII

Change, Potency and Act

I

W E NOW widen our view to take into account the fact of change. That change is a fact needs no proof, but it must be pointed out that it is unintelligible except in relation to being. A formless becoming presents no object to the mind; becoming is either the coming-to-be of something or it is something becoming something else. If Heraclitus or anyone else wanted to say that becoming was everything and that nothing really was, or even that becoming was more fundamental than being, no meaning could in the end be given to these statements. Becoming presupposes being.

Initially change may be supposed to take the form of A B becoming A C while remaining A, or simply of A coming to be or ceasing to be or being replaced by B. But the latter cases really imply a common background which persists. Otherwise A coming to be would be simply a beginning and A ceasing to be simply an ending, while there would be nothing to link the being of A with the being of B. Anything which deserves to be called change, then, involves a situation A B being transformed into a situation A C.

It is evident that change presupposes a successive mode of existence, or time in the widest sense of the word. The meaning of time is sometimes confined to clock-time or astronomical time; in that case, in a situation in which there were no clocks and no astronomical system to be observed, there would be no time. But clocks and the apparent movement of the sun are only means of measuring time; what is measured is fundamentally the same, whatever conceivable means of measuring it there might be and even if it were not measured at all.

Nevertheless we cannot identify time altogether with, for example, the movement that is measured, for the same amount of movement may take place faster or more slowly, that is, in a shorter or a longer amount of time. Time is neither the actual standard of measure adopted nor the concrete change measured; it is a uniform measurability of change, and not only of change but of changeability. In the concrete we have various forms of change, and some supposedly uniform kinds of change are adopted in order to measure the others. Such are clock-movements or the movements of the heavenly bodies. In order to arrive at an abstract conception of time, we have to penetrate deeper than actual changes, whether these be the changes measured or the changes which serve as measures. Time is the quantitative character of the successive continuity which is the condition not simply of actual change but of changeability.

It is in this sense that we should interpret Aristotle's celebrated definition of time as "the number of change according to before and after" ($\dot{\alpha}\varrho\iota\theta\mu\dot{o}\varsigma$ $\varkappa\iota\nu\dot{\eta}\sigma\varepsilon\omega\varsigma$ $\varkappa\alpha\tau\alpha$ $\tau\dot{o}$ $\pi\varrho\dot{o}\tau\varepsilon\varrho o\nu$ $\varkappa\alpha\dot{\iota}$ $\ddot{v}\sigma\tau\varepsilon\varrho o\nu$).[1] Aristotle might seem to be identifying time with the standard employed for measuring it, but he really talks about time as a measure because he wants to distinguish it from the changes measured by it. If such changes have a uniform kind of successiveness independent of the actual rates of change, this is a measure of actual changes but still something to be measured on its own account. The number in the definition is *numerus numeratus*, not *numerus numerans*.

Time, then, is a successive quantitative character arising from changeability, and its measure measures the rate of actual changes. There is still time where there is change-

[1] Aristotle, *Physics*, iv, 11, 219, b, 2.

ability but no actual change, although a stretch of time in which there is no change can only be experienced as a unity. Here the intuitions of folklore come to the support of philosophy with all the stories of unaccountable lapses of ordinary time when a man is undergoing some extraordinary experience. In a medieval instance of this kind of tale it is precisely when a monk is singing the verse "A thousand years in thy sight are but as yesterday" that he becomes absorbed in his meditations and walks out into the forest, finding on his return that three centuries have elapsed. Such stories express imaginatively the truth that time is correlative with changeability but its lapse can be appreciated only through actual change. It is interesting to note that Aristotle himself illustrates this point with a similar legend, referring to people of Sardis who were said to have slept with the heroes and to have been unaware of the passing of time.[1] All changeable things, then, are subject to time, and only the absolutely unchangeable is timeless.

Time is evidently a real characteristic of changeable things and is the source of the relations of before, after and simultaneity. But time is equally evidently not really distinct from the being of changeable things. It is inherent in being changeable and appears, indeed, from a metaphysical point of view to be a diminution or dissipation of being; in so far as a thing possesses its being more completely the less it is subject to change and the more it is what it is all at once. Yet, given imperfection and changeability, time is a necessary field of positive development and fulfilment.

Change may be either discrete or continuous. The concept of discrete change raises no special problem, but the possibility of continuous change is questioned by the type of argument contained in the paradoxes of Zeno. In traversing any distance you must first reach halfway; before reaching halfway, you must reach a quarter of the way, and so on; it appears that you can never make a start. The

[1] Aristotle, *Physics*, iv, 11, 218, 23–5.

fleet-footed Achilles can never overtake the sluggish tortoise, for, when he arrives at the point which the tortoise has left, the tortoise is at a point some distance in advance; when Achilles has arrived at this point, the tortoise is farther on, and so forth. The flying arrow is really at rest, for at any moment it occupies a space equal to its own length, and that is to be at rest. Zeno of Elea deserves every credit for having brightened philosophy by the invention of these ancient puzzles, but, if we bear in mind the difference between the logical and the real order, it is not very difficult to resolve them. If there is continuous change, stages in the change and moments in the time taken can be designated by an act of mind to any extent desired, but these stages and moments do not exist as distinct entities. They are only logically distinct from the continuous process of change and time; reality in its own right belongs only to the beginning and end of the change, the being with which it begins and the being with which it terminates, as well as to the process taken as a whole, for the process is a real unity of becoming. Hence the concept of continuous change involves no contradiction.

It would be a mistake, however, to suppose that we could settle the question by asserting that we observe continuous change. The invention of the cinematograph has fortunately provided a clear example of the fact that continuous change is not a matter of direct observation. For, whatever may have been the case with the earliest examples of this device, it is now possible to watch a film without observing any difference from the kinds of change that we suppose to be continuous. Yet we are in fact watching a rapid succession of still photographs. If, therefore, the other changes which we suppose to be continuous were successions of discrete changes of the same order of rapidity as obtains in the cinematograph, we should have no means of knowing the difference. We cannot, consequently, assert on mere grounds of observation that any change is continuous.

When we reflect on this question more in principle, we have to acknowledge that awareness is primarily an awareness of being. What we are primarily aware of is, then, a succession of states of being. Armed with the notions of being and of discrete change, we can conceptually fill in the intervals of a uniform succession of changes and arrive at the supposition of continuous change. But continuous change is a conceptual construction, not an object of observation, and we may be deceived in supposing it to obtain in reality as we might be if we thought that a film was really continuous. Hence, while, in opposition to Zeno, we should assert that continuous change involves no contradiction, we must also admit that its actual occurrence in any instance demands proof.

2

In coming to Aristotle's definition of movement or change (κίνησις) as the actuality of what is in potency as in potency (ἡ τοῦ δυνάμει ὄντος ἐντελέχεια ᾗ τοιοῦτον)[1] we make contact with his theory of act and potency. And this is the proper place to do so. For, although the meaning of these terms can be usefully extended beyond situations of change, they clearly derive their fundamental meaning from change, and any extension of their meaning derives its point from this. Moreover, from this stage onwards, we shall have more to do with Aristotle, for he has little to say about being as being but much to say about becoming. Yet his metaphysic is not a mere metaphysic of becoming but a metaphysic of becoming in terms of being.

The concepts of act and potency arise from a consideration of a changing thing. For change is not a mere arbitrary addition and subtraction of being. It is not true that anything can become anything else. What things actually are is the actual determination of their being, but what they are able to be is a range of determinability which is wider but

[1] Aristotle, *Physics*, iii, 1, 201, a, 10–11.

not indefinite. Hence a changeable thing has to be described as a subject of potentialities, some of which are actualized at any given moment, while others may have been actualized in the past and others may be actualized in the future, and yet others may never be actualized at all. A lump of clay has a certain actual shape and size: it might potentially be moulded into a model of a statue of Mars or Venus; perhaps it is actually used for a model of the statue of the first Mayor of Eastbourne; nevertheless it retains its potentialities of being moulded into other shapes including an indefinite number of shapes which it never actually receives. Here are the primary meanings of potentiality and actuality, or potency and act, potency as passive determinability and act as actual determination.

But, if we may anticipate the discussion of causality in order to present an adequate account of Aristotle's doctrine of potency and act, things are also in dynamic relationship with one another. In given circumstances things produce effects on other things. Even when they are not actually producing such effects, they are in potentiality to doing so when the proper circumstances occur. Here is another meaning of potency as active power. In our own language it is natural to distinguish passive and active potencies as potentialities and powers; Aristotle distinguishes δύναμις τοῦ πάσχειν and τοῦ ποιεῖν.[1]

An ambiguity appears at this stage. For we often and naturally speak of things as producing effects in themselves, immanent and not transeunt activities. We speak of acts of thinking and acts of choosing. Aristotle is perfectly well aware of this and, although his general principle is that, while the actuality of a passive potentiality belongs to the subject of potentiality, the actuality of an active potentiality accrues to the thing affected by it, he admits that there are cases in which a thing may by its active potentiality affect itself as if it were other. An active power may be ἀρχή

---

[1] Aristotle, *Metaphysics*, θ, 1, 1046a, 19–20.

μεταβολῆς ἐν ἄλλῳ ἢ ᾗ ἄλλο.[1] But, if this is so, and it certainly is so, does not the clear-cut distinction between active and passive power disappear? The actualization of a passive potentiality requires the intervention of an external cause, but the activity of an active power does not take place without an external stimulus; otherwise it would always be active in that way. It would seem that the actualization of a potentiality always calls for the collaboration of the subject of potentiality with external circumstances. How then do we distinguish activity and passivity?

There can be no doubt that the distinction between activity and passivity is not as clear-cut as Aristotle would have liked to make it. Yet it is a familiar distinction, and it would be rash to abolish it without more inquiry. Its full explanation really demands a teleological consideration which Aristotle does not introduce at this point. We think of a thing and of its potentialities as active when it is changing in the direction of greater development and fulfilment and as passive when the change is in the opposite direction, but in any change both the potentialities of the changing thing and the powers of the external stimuli belong to the sum of the causal antecedents.

So much for potentiality as Aristotle conceives it. Since actuality corresponds both to passive potentialities and active powers, a parallel distinction can be made between actualization and causal activity. A similar comment is required. To the extent that actual determination takes place in the direction of development and fulfilment we think of the subject as causally active in it, and in the last resort the subject is always part of the sum of the causal antecedents of its determinations. In a closer connection with Aristotle's text we have to distinguish ἐνέργεια and ἐντελέχεια, which can both be translated in various contexts as act, activity, actuality and actualization. Apart from the special meaning of ἐντελέχεια as a substantial nature, of which this is not the

---

[1] *Metaphysics*, θ, 1, 1946a, 11.

place to speak, there is no very systematic distinction in Aristotle, but ἐνέργεια tends to suggest activity and imperfect actualization while ἐντελέχεια suggests full realization.

Nevertheless Aristotle defines change as the ἐντελέχεια of the potential as such. But the term is appropriate, for the potential as such is the changeable and the full realization of changeability is actual change. After what we have said in general about act and potency this description of change becomes intelligible. A reading of *Metaphysics*, θ, which is Aristotle's systematic treatise on act and potency, will contribute an enlargement of understanding of the whole subject. Whatever may be the defects and ambiguities of Aristotle's doctrine, we should be unjust if we thought it less than a contribution of value to the exact description of change and of changing things. In metaphysics we must go on to ask about the ontological status of potentialities and powers, but this will come most appropriately in the discussion of substance.

This is rather the moment to issue a warning that in the Aristotelian tradition the distinction of potency and act is frequently applied in the logical order as well as in the real. In the logical order the distinction becomes exactly equivalent to the distinction between determinable and determinant. A genus is to a specific difference in the logical relationship of potency to act. Hence we have to be careful to discern in what mode the terms are being used lest we be tempted to multiply real distinctions where there is only a logical distinction and relation.

In the logical relationship of determinable and determinant the determinant is unambiguously an addition of greater positivity to the determinable; it is more to be an animal than simply to be a living thing. In the ordinary metaphysical relationship of potency and act the act is equally an addition of positivity but, since the potency is not a mere logical determinable but a power which in a sense demands activity and fulfilment, degrees of actualization may be above or below what is regarded as a normal development of the potential subject. The case is somewhat different when the terms are applied to essence and existence. In the logical sense of essence and existence we may analogically describe existence as the determinant and act of essence, although the relation is not exactly similar to the relation of determinant and determinable which obtains between aspects of the essence. When we come to the Thomistic metaphysical distinction which for the sake of clearness we call the distinction of being and quiddity, being is still described as the act of the quiddity because being is the principle of positivity and quiddity is the principle of limitation, but, if we were to make a similar analogical application of the concepts of determinable and determinant, being would be the determinable and quiddity the determinant. Hence St. Thomas himself speaks of a determination of being by quiddity but hastens to add that this is not like the determination of potency by act but rather the other way round.[1] Thus the application of the notions of potency and act to the distinction of being and quiddity is analogical and has to be made with the difference as well as the similarity in mind. That is why it is a mistake to treat the problem of essence and existence as an instance of a more general distinction of potency and act; the proper method to follow is to treat it first for its own sake and in its own terms and only later, when the ordinary meanings of potency and act can be appropriately introduced, to consider how far and in what way these notions can be applied to it.

3

The concept of possibility appears first in a logical context. We know that certain things actually exist and that others have actually existed, and we may be able to infer

---

[1] "Non sic determinatur esse per aliud sicut potentia per actum sed magis sieut actus per potentiam" (St. Thomas Aquinas, *De Potentia*, q. 7, a. ii, ad 9).

that other things will actually exist. By the same token we know that anything incompatible with the things of whose actual existence we are aware does not exist; it is impossible by reference to what we know. Bacon and egg were the only dish that I had for breakfast this morning; hence I know that I did not have sausages or, to put it less naturally, that the sausages I had for breakfast this morning did not exist and could not have existed on account of their incompatibility with my actual breakfast. There is obviously another sense in which I might have had sausages for breakfast this morning, but we may leave this aside for the moment.

Beyond the small area of reality lit up by my means of information there is a vast field belonging to past, present and future in which I do not know what exists and what does not exist. It is a field of possibility in which I do not know what possibilities are realized and what are not. Of course there is also a penumbra surrounding the area of certain knowledge and obtaining a partial illumination from my estimates of probability. What I know makes certain possibilities more probable and certain other possibilities less probable. Probability, however, is an exclusively logical notion. To say that anything is probable is always an abbreviated way of saying that the available evidence gives it a certain measure of likelihood. It would be meaningless to say that anything was probable in itself; things in themselves either are or are not. The real world contains no class of probable existents.

It is also true that the real world contains no class of possible existents, but the notion of possibility takes another form in which it has a kind of application to the real world which the notion of probability can never acquire. This is the sense in which I might have had sausages for breakfast this morning. By this I mean that no absurdity or contradiction is inherent in the idea of my having sausages for breakfast. Anything which contains an internal contradiction, like a square circle, is intrinsically impossible;

anything from which contradiction is absent is intrinsically possible. In this sense of intrinsic possibility everything that actually exists must be possible. "Ab esse ad posse valet illatio." Thus the class of the intrinsically possible becomes an immensely wide class of which the class of actual existents is a small part. We are once again within measurable distance of the fallacy exemplified by the mode of thinking of the ontological argument, the fallacy of supposing that the world consists of a vast multitude of possible things some of which actually exist while others do not.

In order to dispose of this fallacy for the last time we must make our language more precise in a way similar to that required by our earlier discussion of actual existence. To say that a horse exists means that some existent thing takes the form of a horse. What does it mean to say that a centaur does not exist? It is not enough to say that no existent thing takes the form of a centaur, for no existent thing is no more a real subject of predicates than the alleged possible centaur. Remembering Plato's reduction of negation to otherness, we have rather to say that we are making an assertion about the whole universe: everything that exists is other than a centaur.

What then shall we make of possibility and impossibility? Impossibility turns out to be the more fundamental notion. In the first sense in which we spoke of possibility and impossibility, to say that something is impossible means that the character of some known existents entails that this does not exist or, to make the translation complete, that the character of some known existents entails that everything that exists is other than this. That about which we know no such entailment remains possible in the corresponding sense of possibility. These translations serve to make clear how this sense of possibility and impossibility is relative to our actual knowledge.

To say that anything is intrinsically impossible means that reality has a general character which entails the non-existence of this. For example, a square circle is intrinsically impossible because it is a general character of reality that, if anything is a circle, it is not square, and this entails that everything that exists is other than a square circle. The intrinsically possible is simply that whose realization is not excluded by any general character of fact. To say that anything is intrinsically possible means that all the general characters of reality are other than any which would entail that everything that exists was other than this.

Thus whatever we say about the possible or the impossible can be translated into statements about the character of particular facts or the general character of fact. So, for the last time, we conclude that there is no need to postulate a mysterious class of possibilities halfway between being and not-being. The real world contains no halfway house between being and not-being.

But, it is sometimes said, even if possibilities are nothing in themselves, do they not require a foundation in fact other than the finite and changing things of which we are aware in experience? For possibilities possess a timeless validity. This, however, seems to be putting the cart before the horse, for it is only when we recognize that there is absolute and timeless being that we are entitled to assert that there are absolute and timeless possibilities. The timeless validity of the intrinsically possible is not, therefore, a foundation of a theistic philosophy but a consequence of the recognition of absolute being. The case is different when we point out that actual fact as experienced by us manifests general characters which are timelessly valid and seek a real foundation for such timeless truths. Here we are starting not from the merely possible but from the actual, and this consideration, familiar in the thought of St. Augustine, is relevant to the building up of a theistic philosophy. The status of the possible, however, must always be dependent on what we suppose actual fact to be.

It should be added that our positive knowledge of intrinsic

possibility is, apart from the cases when we can argue from actual fact to the possibility of that kind of fact, much more dubious than we might suppose it to be. For only an exhaustive knowledge of the nature of anything we are inclined to believe to be possible could entitle us to assert dogmatically that there is no general character of fact which entails its non-existence. In anything of which we have not an exhaustive knowledge there may be a contradiction which we have not discovered.

A passing mention is all that is deserved by the attempt to attribute some sort of reality to the possible by saying that it exists in those minds which can conceive it and in the power of those agents which could bring it into existence. To say that a thing exists in thought is only a misleading way of saying that the thought of it exists; it confers no reality on the contents of the thought. In the same way, to say that a thing exists in the power which could bring it about is only a misleading way of saying that some existent thing could bring it about; the thing itself remains as non-existent as before.

Sometimes, however, we need a terminology in which to express the extent to which the conditions of realizing a possibility are present. The scholastics distinguished active power from activity as *actus primus* from *actus secundus*. An active power on the threshold of activity was said to be *in actu primo proximo ad agendum*; otherwise it was *in actu primo remoto*. So also a possibility might be said to be *in potentia remota* or *in potentia proxima* according to the extent to which the conditions of its realization were already verified. Such a scale of degrees of possibility in the real order is analogous to degrees of probability in the logical order and can be readily understood without the risk of supposing it to be a scale of degrees of coming to be; what exist in greater or less measure are the conditions of the existence of things and not the things themselves.

CHAPTER VIII

Substance

I

THE LOGICAL distinction between a subject-predicate proposition and a relational proposition has been much emphasized in recent times. The distinction is not altogether clear-cut; all propositions are relational, for all exhibit a unity in difference, and all possess a subject and a predicate, for a relation is predicated of the referent. Nevertheless there is a genuine discrimination to be made between propositions in which the predicate is a quality or activity intrinsic to the subject and those in which the predicate is a relation of the subject to something outside it. Moreover inference in terms of the properties of relations yields a different and no less valid kind of calculus of reasoning from inference in terms of the relation of subject and predicate alone, such as Aristotle made the basis of his main theory of reasoning.

It is not difficult to see that the special character of the logical relation of subject and predicate bears an analogy to the metaphysical relation of substance and attribute or accident. Hence the suggestion has been made that, just as Aristotle overemphasized the subject-predicate relation in his logic, so he at least overemphasized the importance of the substance-accident relation in his metaphysics. Critics have even gone to the length of suggesting that the whole substance-accident relation is an illegitimate projection onto the ontological plane of the logical relation of subject and predicate.

On the other side we might equally suggest that the subject-predicate relation is a logical reflection of the structure of fact in the relation of substance and attribute. Obviously it is applied in many cases where no one would suppose that the subject is a real substance, but our proneness to use this logical form might be a result of our having frequently to talk about real substances and their attributes. As far as these conjectures go, neither side can claim an advantage; the question can only be decided by an examination of the relevant facts in order to see whether the relation of substance and attribute can be properly applied to them.

The chief relevant fact is the situation in which, as it would be described in commonsense language and with a commonsense degree of ambiguity, a thing changes while still remaining the same thing. The same water is first cold and then hot; the same plant is first small and then large; the same dog is first growling and then wagging its tail. The case which is nearest to us is that of ourselves. We have changed in every way through the years; even at the moment our thoughts and feelings are changing; yet each of us will say without hesitation that he is still the same self that he has been through all these changes. Alice's doubts about her identity when interrogated by the caterpillar after her experiences in Wonderland only serve to emphasize the truth that, even in similar circumstances, we should have no such doubts.

Here Hume raises his voice and tells us that there is no mystery about the identity of the self through change, for there is no identity of any single real factor. Each of us is a series and nothing more; to say that we had first this experience and then another is merely to say that both these experiences belong to the same series which is the history of a self. Those for whom Bradley's gorgeous piece of rhetoric about the group of onions on a non-existent rope is not a sufficient, because not a sufficiently analytic, refutation of the

Humian conception of the self[1] must inspect what Hume precisely asserts and the grounds upon which he asserts it. What he says is clear enough.

> If any impression gives rise to the idea of self, that impression must continue invariably the same, thro' the whole course of our lives; since self is suppos'd to exist after that manner. But there is no impression constant and invariable. . . . For my part, when I enter most intimately into what I call *myself*, I always stumble on some particular perception or other, of heat or cold, light or shade, love or hatred, pain or pleasure. I never can catch *myself* at any time without a perception, and never can observe anything but the perception.[2]

We see, therefore, that Hume is looking for some concrete object which he can identify with the self and which can be observed in independence of the actual flow of experience, and, since he can find no such concrete object, he denies the reality of a permanent self. That no such independent impression of the self occurs we may readily admit, and no reasonable person would claim that it does. The real claim of the Aristotelian tradition is that the self is observed in and through its activities. So Aristotle himself says that "in the order of thought activities and actions are prior to powers" (πρότερον γὰρ εἰσι τῶν δυνάμεων αἱ ἐνέργειαι καὶ αἱ πράξεις κατὰ τὸν λόγον)[3]. Aquinas says that "that of which the understanding is first aware is its object; secondly, it is aware of the act by which it is aware of the object; and through the act it is aware of itself, whose fulfilment it is to understand" ("id quod primo cognoscitur ab intellectu humano est huiusmodi obiectum: et secundario cognoscitur

---

[1] F. H. Bradley, *Ethical Studies*, 2nd ed., Oxford, 1927, pp. 36–40.
[2] Hume, *Treatise of Human Nature*, ed. Selby-Bigge, bk. i, pt. iv, s. 6, pp. 251–2.
[3] Aristotle, *De Anima*, ii, 4, 415a, 19–20.

ipse actus quo cognoscitur obiectum; et per actum cognoscitur ipse intellectus, cuius est perfectio ipsum intelligere ").[1]

What we are claiming, then, is not that the self is a concrete object to be observed either along with or independently of the variations of our actual experience but that, when we reflect on our experience, we are simultaneously aware of an element of permanence as well as of variations within it. If we cannot think of the self apart from experience, it is equally impossible, for it would be an equally illegitimate abstraction, to think of experiences simply as atomic events in succession. "A sensation of blue occurs" is not an adequate translation of "I am aware of blue." The serial self proposed by Hume is merely a succession of abstractions; our experience in the concrete is of an identical self in a succession of actual states. In this sense we claim that an element of permanence in ourselves and in the changing persons and things with which we are in contact is obvious; what is not obvious is the analysis of this concrete unity of change and permanence. The metaphysical doctrine of substance and attribute is put forward as providing the due analysis of the situation.

2

Our central line of thought is as follows. If a thing undergoes changes of various kinds while still remaining this same thing, in what does its identity consist? Not in what it actually is in the concrete at any given moment, for this is precisely what changes. Nor can it consist in a fully determinate part of what it is at any moment, for then it would not be one thing but two, an unchanging thing in combination with a changing thing. Only when we make use of the notions of potentiality and actuality can we arrive at a clear conception of what a changing thing is. Since its identity is not to be found on the level of complete actuality, it must be sought on the level of potentiality. The permanent

[1] St. Thomas Aquinas, *Summa Theologica*, I, q. 87, art. iii.

element in a thing subject to change must be a principle of potentialities to be made this or that and of powers to act in this or that way in accordance with circumstances. This is what we mean by substance as opposed to the attributes or accidents which are the actual qualities and activities which the thing manifests under specific conditions.

The classical expression of this doctrine is, of course, to be found in Aristotle, but we must look for its primary basis in the *Physics* rather than in the *Metaphysics*. In the *Metaphysics* Aristotle is largely concerned with substance in the secondary sense, which is the essential nature of a species, and he accordingly discusses how we may envisage the defining characteristics of a class of substances. This is a matter of logic rather than of ontology, and, even when in the *Metaphysics* Aristotle deals with substance in the primary sense, the individual subsistent thing, his attention is still mainly directed towards logical problems. The singular, or first substance, can only be the subject of a sentence; it cannot be a genuine predicate. General terms, on the other hand, are primarily predicates and acquire their real application when they are predicated of singulars. All this could be true if the distinction between substance and attribute were merely a logical distinction between the singular and the general term. We must look elsewhere in order to see whether these logical truths reflect anything of importance in the structure of fact.

That we should have to look at the *Physics* is not to be wondered at if the real distinction of substance and accident is an explanation of changing things, for the subject of the *Physics* is being as changeable. At any rate we find what we want in Aristotle's conception of a nature ($\varphi \acute{v} \sigma \iota \varsigma$). The opening sentences of Book II of the *Physics* distinguish an artefact from a natural thing. An artefact has no intrinsic principle of unity; it is a combination of things designed to fulfil a human purpose extrinsic to the characters of its components. A natural thing possesses an intrinsic unity and an intrinsic principle of activity, for "a nature is a principle and source of change and rest in that to which it belongs" (ὡς οὔσης τῆς φύσεως ἀρχῆς τινὸς καὶ αἰτίας τοῦ κινεῖσθαι καὶ ἠρεμει ἐν ᾧ ὑπαρχει).[1] The behaviour of natural things is not less teleological than that of artefacts, but their teleology is intrinsic; they tend towards a natural fulfilment or entelechy.

Aristotle goes on to show that there is no contradiction between natural necessity and natural teleology (ii, 8–9). Things act according to observable laws, but these laws become intelligible as manifesting the tendencies of things towards their natural fulfilment. Hence what a thing is and what a thing tends to be are both, from different points of view, the sources of its activity. In Aristotelian causal terminology the formal, final and efficient causes come together in the end. Aristotle's teleology in principle, therefore, however defective some of its applications may be, is not a fanciful imputation of anthropomorphic purposes to natural things but a standpoint from which the actual behaviour of things may be made progressively more intelligible.

According to Aristotle's doctrine of substance, then, the ultimate subject in a changing thing is a principle of activity, of potentialities and powers which are variously actualized in different circumstances. It is the dynamic aspect inherent in the notion of φύσις or nature which makes this an ontological doctrine and not merely a logical discrimination of subject and predicate. As long as this dynamic aspect remains in the forefront of attention, the significance and importance of the doctrine are clear; if it is overshadowed or forgotten, the meaning of substance becomes dubious or is lost.

3

Now the preoccupation of the later Middle Ages with logic seems to have had precisely the effect that the formal

[1] Aristotle, *Physics*, ii, 1, 192b, 20–22.

logical aspect of substance overshadowed its dynamic and ontological aspect. Hence the failure to appreciate its significance from the seventeenth century onwards. Descartes has been initiated into Aristotelian philosophy, but he completely misunderstood the doctrine of substance, and it would be an insult to his intelligence to suppose that the fault lay entirely with him and not at all with his instructors. His interpretation was to identify substance with a fundamental actual attribute, so that the substance of mind was thought and the substance of matter was extension. The whole point of the notion of substance is thus lost.

Locke retains the name of substance for the underlying principle of unification which he admits to be necessary in order to explain why we associate numerous and various qualities with the same subject. But substance, as Locke conceives it, is not discovered by an ontological analysis of changing fact; it is inferred as a support of qualities and activities.

So that if anyone will examine himself concerning his notion of pure substance in general, he will find he has no other idea of it at all, but only a supposition of he knows not what support of such qualities which are capable of producing simple ideas in us; which qualities are commonly called "accidents."[1]

Hence, as the nature of substance is unknown, it cannot serve to explain anything except what it was originally invoked to explain. In particular, the unity of personality through time cannot be explained by a unity of substance; if there were two mutually exclusive chains of experience and memory, there would be two personalities in the same organism whatever might be the case with the unity of substance.

[1] Locke, *Essay Concerning Human Understanding*, bk. ii, ch. xxiii, §2.

It is not surprising that philosophers should feel uneasy with so artificial a notion as Locke had of substance, and it was natural enough that Berkeley should abolish the notion of material substance. The material world consisted wholly in what Locke had called simple ideas; things were merely groups of ideas which commonly occurred in association, like the colour, the smell and the taste of an orange. But Berkeley acknowledged an immediate awareness of the self as mind, a self which was active in its awareness of ideas and in its communion with other minds. This might have been a clue to the rediscovery of substance, but Berkeley did not think of applying it outside the sphere of mind.

Hume, as usual, paid no attention to what was constructive in Berkeley but carried the negative aspects in Locke's philosophy to their logical conclusion. The idea of permanent substance was dismissed from the sphere of mind as from that of matter and replaced by the conception of serial continuity. Changing things ceased to be; there were only changes of things, or rather of impressions and ideas, of which each was a self-contained atomic fact.

It cannot be said that more recent philosophy has contributed much to the understanding of substance. Kant's attempted rehabilitation of substance on the phenomenal level took it as a principle for unifying phenomena rather than in its dynamic aspect. This was inevitable, for there can be no real activity in the shadow-world of phenomena. The transcendental self, no doubt, was active behind the scenes, but it could not become an object of the theoretical reason.

Only in our own times has an attempt been made to bring the active self into full recognition again, for the *Existenz* of the existentialists, especially as described by Jaspers, is the self as the source of its states and activities, and it is emphasized that this is the primary character of the self. *Existenz* is Kant's transcendental ego brought once again into the sphere of speculative philosophy although still regarded as outside the range of the object-thinking of the sciences. The Kantian presuppositions of existentialism are made even more evident by the fact that this active character is regarded as belonging exclusively to persons and is not extended to corporeal things, but a reading of what Jaspers has to say about *Existenz* can be helpful as an awakening to the possibility of grasping the meaning of substance. In the Aristotelian tradition, however, the distinction of substance and accident is the result of a metaphysical analysis of changing being in general, and we want to see whether it can be upheld in this full range of application.

4

A vague misgiving may arise from the difference between things as we perceive them and things as we think them if we think them in terms of substance and attribute. The world as we perceive it is a field of rich and varied actualization. Now we are asked to think of things as being primarily potentialities and powers, of whose interaction perceptible qualities are the comparatively superficial result. That, in general, we should have to modify our outlook in passing from the logical to the real order should not, however, surprise us. Moreover we do not simply perceive attributes; we perceive things under their actual attributes. A thing with its changing actualizations is the object of our metaphysical analysis, and if in the light of this analysis we have to distinguish powers from actualizations, we are not really dividing the thing from its qualities and activities. The thing which is permanently a unity of potentialities and powers is itself the same variously actualized thing which we perceive from moment to moment. There is a real metaphysical distinction of substance and attribute, but this is not a distinction of concrete things any more than is the distinction of being and quiddity. The substance with its actual attributes is one concrete thing, but the distinction of substance and attribute has to be made in order that a changing thing should be intelligible.

We must also be careful not to logicize reality by regarding all predicates as corresponding to real attributes. If we did this, we should be turning substance into a pure form of singularity devoid even of potential being, for potentialities and powers are themselves expressed as predicates. This would be precisely Locke's unintelligible conception of an unknown somewhat which serves in a mysterious way as a subject and substratum of the powers, qualities and activities which we attribute to a thing. The logical distinction of subject and predicate doubtless reflects in its way the distinction of substance and attribute, but there is no exact correspondence between them. The ontological distinction which the nature of a changing thing compels us to make is between a unity of potentialities and powers on the one hand and actual qualities and activities on the other. Powers and faculties are not mysterious entities halfway between substance and full actuality; if they had to be regarded in this way, the scorn with which they have often been treated by modern philosophers would be well merited. For they would then be both actual attributes and yet merely potential, which is a contradiction. Our contention is that they are aspects under which we partially grasp the nature of the substance which manifests the activities corresponding to them. To assert a real distinction between substance and powers is impossible, although the assertion is made by many scholastic philosophers, for the substance becomes featureless and cannot give rise to powers while the powers become mere possibilities, in isolation from the substance to which they belong.

But, it may be said, this is only to push the difficulty one step farther back, for, if substance is a unity of potentialities and powers, the same objection can be made to regarding it as a really distinct element of fact. We have been protesting all along against the tendency to suppose that the world consists of possible things which do not exist as well as actual things which do exist. Have we ourselves fallen into the trap at last by canonizing an element of mere possibility under the name of substance? If we maintain that we are not guilty of this error, it is because we are not attributing independent concrete reality to substance apart from its accidents and because substance combines its powers in the positive reality of individual thinghood.

The case is parallel with that of being and quiddity. Quiddity is a principle of limitation, and no thing could be a mere principle of limitation. But quiddity is not asserted to be an independent thing; a finite thing is a unity of being and quiddity. Moreover quiddity is individual, and individuality, although not a content of being, is something positive. Hence individual quiddity is sufficiently positive to be a real principle within the unity of the concrete thing composed of being and quiddity. In an analogous way substance is a principle of potentiality, but it is not asserted to be a concrete thing apart from its attributes. Moreover, as it is the fundamental subject, individuality belongs primarily to it and accrues to its attributes through it. Hence, as individual, substance is sufficiently positive to be a real principle within the unity of the concrete thing composed of substance and attributes.

In a finite and changing thing, therefore, being is limited by an individual quiddity which is primarily characterized by potentialities and powers. Being is enlarged and quiddity specified by the varying actualizations of these potentialities and powers under different conditions. Although in the logical order of essence actuality is prior and potentiality is intelligible only by relation to actuality, in the order of being, when we are concerned with finite and changing being, potentiality is prior and is the source of varying actuality. Awkward as it is to express these matters clearly in human language, which was not invented by metaphysicians and has to be rather violently adapted to their purposes, what we have been trying to express as intelligibly as possible is the necessary outcome of reflection on finite and changing being.

5

Where do we find substances in the world of experience? The changing thing with which we are best acquainted is, of course, the self, and we have already had occasion to appeal to the experience of the self as witness to an identity through change and time. But the self is really an extremely complicated kind of substance, for we are organisms as well as minds. Mind manifests one characteristic kind of continuity and identity through time, but the continuity and identity of the organism appears to be of a different kind. It is not an identity of the particles of matter of which we are composed, for we are credibly informed by the scientists that these are in a condition of constant flux. It is rather an identity of structure, or perhaps we ought to say a similarity and continuity of structure, for the changes which take place between infancy and old age are too obvious to need mentioning in detail.

If we look for an easier example, we might refer to the elementary particles of matter as the simplest kind of substances. Unfortunately we are now faced with the difficulty that we do not know what the elementary particles of matter are. In the past, as the derivation of the name shows, atoms were thought to be elementary; now they turn out to have a complex structure. In my early youth they were said to be composed of protons and electrons, but I have since gathered that various other enigmatic components have been added by the physicists from time to time. Far be it from me to offer any opinion on these matters or to guess what physicists of the future will find to be the components of what they now provisionally regard as elementary. Nor can we conjecture what will happen if the electron is split as the atom has been.

At any rate we may say that, whatever the elementary constituents of matter may be, they will be the simplest kind of substances. And now what of atoms, and what of chemical molecules, and what of biological organisms? Are these to be considered as combinations of substances or single substances in which the substances of their components are absorbed? Neither description seems satisfactory. All these things seem to be more than mere aggregates, and yet it does not appear that their constituents wholly lose their identity.

We should first ask whether we are entitled to a simple answer to the question whether this is one substance or many. When dealing with enumeration we pointed out that things could be unambiguously enumerated only when they were both similar and mutually exclusive. If a part deserved the same description as the whole of which it was a part, whole and part could not be enumerated together. Everything points to this being the case with the notion of substance, for the criterion of a substance is a distinctive unity of behaviour. An atom appears to have a distinctive character and activity, but its components do not seem to have lost their own character and activity. A chemical combination appears to be a genuine novelty in the realm of substance, but the atoms seem to continue in many ways to act as before. An organism is an eminently distinctive type of agent, with its capacity for self-preservation, development and reproduction, yet its physical and chemical constituents do not seem to have altogether lost their independence.

The facts, therefore, seem to demand that we should acknowledge that a thing may be one substance and many substances at the same time. Hence the question, how many substances are there in the world, is meaningless. Wherever we find a distinctive mode of activity which is not the sum of the activities of the components of the thing, we rightly recognize a distinctive kind of substance, but we should also be willing to admit that, if the components retain their specific activities, they have not lost their substantial identity. Transcendental unity, as we have already pointed out, is an analogous term. Consequently, since substance is the fundamental principle of finite and changing thing-hood, it should not be surprising that a thing or a sub-stance should be in one respect one and in other respects many. In order to explain the substantial unity of an atom or of a molecule or of an organism we do not need to invoke some entirely new principle of unity; a vital principle in this sense, for instance, is a gratuitous piece of mythology. The unity of a compound substance is the respect under which its constituents have become a unity of activity; its multi-plicity lies in the respects in which they have retained their separate character. This again is genuine Aristotelianism, for what Aristotle acknowledged in such cases was not a new agent somehow infused into the compound but a new form ($\mu o \varrho \varphi \acute{\eta}$), a unity of structure which made the compound more than an aggregate. It remains, however, that the substantial unity of a thinking mind with an organism raises quite special problems of analysis, for no unity of material parts can conceivably be the source of thought and a new con-stituent is needed which must yet be seen as entering into genuine unity with the organism. But a specific dis-cussion of the body-mind problem does not belong to general metaphysics.

CHAPTER IX

Value

I

THE ARISTOTELIAN conception of good or value as residing in the fulfilment of natural capacity arises at once from the discussion of substance, but, from the point of view of contemporary philosophy, some preliminaries are needed. Terms expressive of absolute value are a puzzle to the followers of Hume. The relative values of economics can be interpreted easily enough in terms of what people are ready to pay for things, but, when we say that things are good in themselves, as when we say that actions are right in themselves, the case is different. Ethical and aesthetic values are not observable qualities in the sense admitted by Hume; there is no distinctive impression or idea corresponding with the goodness of a man, the rightness of an action or the beauty of a work of art. Nor can these notions be reduced with any show of plausibility to the purely formal linguistic or symbolic status which has sometimes been assigned to logic and mathematics. Value-judgments appear to assert something about the real character of things. Yet, within the limits set by logical positivism, it is exceedingly difficult to say what they assert.

Hence it is sometimes alleged that value-judgments assert nothing at all but are instances of the emotive use of language. They do not even assert the existence of an emotion; they are direct expressions of it. That language has an emotive use which is other than assertoric is clear enough. "X is a liar" and "X is a rotten liar" are sentences which make the same assertion; the addition of "rotten" is merely an expression of your justifiable dislike of lying. It is also true that sentences which appear to assert something may turn out to make no easily discoverable assertion or even no assertion at all. This is familiar in poetry. Was Keats trying to assert anything when he said "'Beauty is truth, truth beauty'—that is all ye know on earth, and all ye need to know"? It is certainly not easy to decide what he was intending to assert, for, if his words are taken literally, it is too obvious that beauty and truth are not identical and that, even if they were, this would not be the only available or necessary piece of information on earth. A reasonable person will interpret the passage rather as an expression of Keats' feelings about truth and beauty and nothing more. No literary critic, plainly, would waste his time considering the possible validity of the literal paraphrase which we have just made.

There can be no doubt that value-terms lend themselves to emotive use and that ostensible assertions about value are often no more than expressions of feeling. It does not follow that they are always such, and it must be remembered that to every expression of feeling corresponds a reflex statement asserting that someone has that feeling. Even if your cry of "Good shot!" is simply an expression of what you are feeling, the situation has to be described by the statement that you are feeling approval of the stroke made. Consequently the emotive interpretation is not fundamentally different from the theory that value-judgments are statements about emotional attitudes and mean that I or others have feelings of liking, desire and approval or of dislike, aversion and disapproval.

Again there can be no doubt that the good in a general sense is an object of liking, desire and approval and that the bad provokes dislike, aversion and disapproval. If, for example, it is said that someone likes an uncomfortable chair, it means either that he finds comfort in what other

125

people would regard as uncomfortable or that he pursues an ascetic value in the absence of comfort. No one can like the bad precisely as bad or dislike the good precisely as good. But our present business is not to emphasize these truisms; it is to consider the kind of theory which goes no farther and is content with a definition of good as the object of such feelings as desire and approval and of evil as the object of such feelings as aversion and disapproval. Hobbes provides the classical example of a bald statement of this subjectivist view.

> Whatsoever is the object of any man's appetite or desire, that is it which he for his part calleth *good*: and the object of his hate and aversion, *evil*; and of his contempt, *vile* and *inconsiderable*. For these words of good, evil, and contemptible, are ever used with relation to the person that useth them: there being nothing simply and absolutely so; nor any common rule of good and evil, to be taken from the nature of the objects themselves.[1]

Subjectivist theories of value have been the object of vigorous refutation by contemporary philosophers such as Professor G. E. Moore[2] and Dr. A. C. Ewing.[3] The main points are that if, when I say that a thing is good or evil, I mean only that I have a certain attitude or feeling towards it, I can never be wrong except through a failure in introspection and can never be at odds with anyone else on the question. For if another man holds to be evil what I call good, all he means is that he has a different attitude or feeling towards it, which involves no contradiction. But people certainly discuss values as if they were doing something more than comparing notes about their feelings. Even in aesthetic matters it is not usually supposed to be adequate

---

[1] Hobbes, *Leviathan*, pt. i, ch. vi.
[2] G. E. Moore, *Ethics*, London, 1930, pp. 79–169.
[3] A. C. Ewing, *The Definition of Good*, London and New York, 1947, pp. 1–35.

criticism to say that you do not know whether it is good art but you know what you like, and with moral values the claim to objectivity is even clearer. We do not merely dislike cruelty; we think that cruelty is objectively detestable and that, consequently, every one else should detest it also.

To meet this difficulty the subjectivist theory may be emended in the form that good means that of which the majority of men, or the majority of those of our age and civilization, are in favour, while evil means that to which they are opposed. The theory is now no longer purely individualistic but has acquired a measure of quasi-objectivity although value is still construed in terms of feeling. Correct valuation would thus become a matter of statistical inquiry. But that does not seem to correspond any better with what we think ourselves to be discussing when we are discussing values. On this theory aesthetic innovators and moral reformers would be, by definition, wrong, whereas we spontaneously suppose, not that they are always right, but that it is quite possible that they may be right.

The truth is that we cannot help asking why we like this and dislike that. We cannot help asking why other men judge values as they do and whether they are justified in doing so. What we are looking for is some objective character in what is judged to be good or evil. We could not linger in the subjectivist theory unless we gave up this objective quest as hopeless.

2

Dr. Ewing thinks that the necessary transition to objectivity can be made by introducing the notion of fittingness. He defines good as the fitting object of a pro-attitude.[1] That this is a sound definition in the sense that it applies to all of the defined and only to the defined may be admitted, but it does not pass the test that the terms of a definition should

[1] *The Definition of Good*, pp. 145–85.

be logically prior to what is defined. We should all naturally say that a pro-attitude is fitting because its object is good, not that a thing is good because a pro-attitude towards it is fitting. Hence we are still looking for an intrinsic character of value and are compelled to ask wherein it consists.

At this stage we meet G. E. Moore's celebrated doctrine that good is a simple unanalysable quality which we have only to recognize as attaching to certain things and situations. Moore's positive argument for this view is summed up in the sentence: "The most important sense of 'definition' is that in which a definition states what are the parts which invariably compose a certain whole; and in this sense 'good' has no definition because it is simple and has no parts."[1] His supplementary negative argument is a painstaking demolition of the attempts made by various philosophers to define goodness.

While Moore may be right in thinking the meaning of goodness to be intrinsically simple, it does not follow that it cannot be defined in the sense of making it intelligible by exhibiting its necessary relations. The notion of moral obligation, for example, is *sui generis* and irreducible to anything else, but it is made intelligible by defining the kind of situation in which it arises. Individuality we found to be a simple and irreducible notion, but we tried to make it intelligible by discussing the conditions of individuality. The only kind of notion which is absolutely indefinable except in the somewhat Pickwickian sense of ostensive definition by being pointed out is a notion which is not only simple but logically primitive. You cannot define what yellow means except by showing an instance of it, because the notion of yellowness has no logical presuppositions.

Moore actually assimilated good to yellow as simple unanalysable notions, but he soon came to see that there was an important logical difference although he was unable to describe the difference clearly.

[1] *Principia Ethica*, Cambridge, 1903, p. 9.

I can only vaguely express the kind of difference I feel there to be by saying that intrinsic properties [like yellow] seem to *describe* the intrinsic nature of what possesses them in a sense in which predicates of value never do. If you could enumerate *all* the intrinsic properties a given thing possessed, you would have given a *complete* description of it, and would not need to mention any predicates of value it possessed; whereas no description of a given thing could be *complete* which omitted any intrinsic property.[1]

Sir David Ross makes the difference more precise by pointing out that value "seems quite definitely to be based on certain other qualities of its possessors, and not the other qualities on the value" and that it "follows from the *whole* intrinsic nature of its possessors" and may therefore be called "a toti-resultant property".[2]

Hence we may conjecture, with Bosanquet, that goodness, however simple in itself, is complex in its conditions and that "definable, by properties and function, is just what it is, and indefinable—merely designable by pointing—is just what it is not".[3]

3

Returning to Aristotle, we can now ask whether the kind of analysis of value suggested by him does justice to the various ways in which we talk about value. At a first glance his description of the springs of change looks immoderately anthropomorphic. Change is said to presuppose that something by its nature tends towards the possession of something "divine and good and desirable"[4] which it lacks. In the light of Aristotle's doctrine of substance, however,

[1] *Philosophical Studies*, London, 1922, p. 274.
[2] *The Right and the Good*, Oxford, 1930, pp. 121–2.
[3] B. Bosanquet, *Some Suggestions in Ethics*, London, 1919, p. 52.
[4] Aristotle, *Physics*, i, 9, 192, **a,** 17.

we can see that he wants to draw a fairly close analogy between conscious tendency and desire, on the one hand, and on the other the unconscious tendency towards development and fulfilment which he attributes to every substantial nature. That his universal teleology did not turn out in the end to be an adequate tool of scientific investigation need not make us deny its rightful place in the metaphysical analysis of change. Change, from the point of view of its active source, is a tendency towards a natural end or fulfilment, and the end or final cause is "good or apparent good".[1]

Good, then, is the object of desire and approval, and it is a fitting object of desire and approval, but this is because intrinsically it resides in the development and fulfilment of natural potentialities. Good is actuality and actuality is good; degrees of actualization are degrees of goodness or value. The complete good of anything is the fullest possible development of its potentialities in harmony and proportion. But, since everything must be actualized to some extent in order to exist at all, all being has some degree of value: *omne ens est bonum*. Being and value are one in reality, but the notion of value adds to that of being the element of more or less, of degree or quantity in the widest sense.

Such is the primary notion of intrinsic value or good as an end, with which we must contrast instrumental value or good as a means. The distinction is familiar enough. A banknote is a piece of paper with a design which we may or may not regard as aesthetically attractive; the truth is that most of us have scarcely examined the design, for we are interested not in the note's intrinsic value, which is in any case small, but in its instrumental value as something which we can exchange for more solid satisfactions. Even the miser can hardly be supposed to have a passion for the intrinsic value of his coins or banknotes; his curious turn of mind lies in a preference for the power of obtaining satisfactions over

---

[1] Aristotle, *Physics*, ii, 3, 195, a, 26.

their actual enjoyment. On the other hand the insistence of the craftsman on worthy design is a desire to invest what are primarily means or instruments with some of the characteristics of ends, so that man may not lose himself in an uncomely world of means and forget the significance of intrinsic value. Intrinsic value for man must lie in the fulfilment of his nature, of his intellectual powers in knowledge, of his intellectual and sensory powers combined in aesthetic experience, and of his affective nature in friendship and love.

A thinking being can envisage value both in the present and in the future, both in himself and in others. This is the basis of the discrimination, which is directly relevant to ethics, made by Aristotle when he says that "there are three motives of choice and three of avoidance, on the one hand the noble, the expedient and the pleasant and on the other the base, the harmful and the painful".[1] Pleasure arises from the conscious possession of present value, and this is true not only of pleasures of which we approve but also of pleasures of which we disapprove, for we disapprove of the latter not precisely because of what makes them pleasant but on account of the much greater values which they exclude. Even the most perverse and odious of pleasures must be admitted by the philosopher to contain an element of genuine value in, for example, a certain intensity of experience; otherwise it would not be a source of temptation to anyone. Everything that is desired is desired *sub ratione boni*.

The expedient is what is good as a means to future intrinsic good. There may or may not be a conflict between pleasure and expediency; the puritan is the man who thinks that there is always such a conflict, while the hedonist at least implicitly supposes that there cannot be. Neither extreme can be rationally upheld.

Finally the noble is the absolutely good, that which is good in the widest range of reference, not only for the

[1] Aristotle, *Nicomachean Ethics*, ii, 3, 1104, b, 30–32.

individual but for everyone else as well. The word which we render as "noble" is καλόν, which in other contexts means "beautiful" and always conveys the suggestion that moral and aesthetic value coincide at least in their fullest forms. Right action, says Aristotle repeatedly, is for the sake of the noble.

4

What becomes of evil in this account of value? The difficulty has often been raised that, if value consists in degree of being, we can speak of better and less good but never of evil, for this would mean less than nonentity. Since we have already repeated the adage that all being is good, we cannot baldly deny all that is said in this objection. It is true that nothing can be absolutely and completely evil, for everything has some measure of being and, therefore, of value. Nor, if actuality were alone to be considered, would there be anything in the notion of evil except that of a lesser good, but, in accordance with the doctrine of substance, actuality has to be measured in proportion to potentiality. It is from this that evil acquires its force and poignancy. The doctrine of substance, therefore, is of fundamental moment in the theory of value.

A change may be in the direction either of greater or of lesser actualization. Moreover a reduction in actuality may be either a mere lessening of activity or a definite frustration of a natural tendency. On the sensory level pain is the evidence of a frustration or, in Aristotelian language, a privation (στέρησις) of natural activity. Pain has its positive biological function as a warning to the organism and a stimulus to readapt itself in the sequel, but at the moment it is evidence of a negation of natural potentiality. Thus anything whose potentialities are partially frustrated, even though it possesses value to the extent that it is actualized, is in another respect in a condition of disvalue or evil.

Intrinsic evil, therefore, resides not simply in a situation of lesser value but in a definite frustration of natural potentiality or tendency. Furthermore, just as we can speak of instrumental value, so we have to recognize instrumental disvalue. A thing, whatever its intrinsic actuality may be, can be predominantly evil in its effects. Although an earthquake may be a magnificent exhibition of the powers of nature, nevertheless, if it takes place at the site of a city like Lisbon or Messina, we naturally regard it from our human point of view on account of its effects as evil. Effective disvalue attaches typically to the evil will. While we are inclined to pity at least as much as we condemn a man who is his own worst enemy on account of his devotion, say, to Bacchus or to Venus in her more lascivious aspects, we reserve our utter condemnation for the man who spreads suffering and ruin around him and especially for the cruelty which rejoices in doing so.

The theory that evil resides in a negation of being does not, therefore, deserve the reproach that it reduces evil to nothing. A frustration of natural tendency is a significant negation. Equally the source of such frustrations is evil in a still more significant sense. Yet it remains true that no positive degree of being as such is evil.

The concept of importance suggests itself here, for it is related to value while covering both value and disvalue. The sources of great good and the sources of great evil are equally important. If we sometimes ask to be delivered from great men, we are thinking of the harm which one kind of great man does. The great conquerors of history, for example, have done immeasurably more harm than good. But it would be a petty revenge of less powerful personalities to deny their greatness when their day is over. That is a point on which Nietzsche is instructive. In our own day, whatever may have been the physical and psychological defects from which Adolf Hitler suffered, to overlook his demonic force is both a stupidity in itself and a dishonour to those who stood out against him and only just succeeded in defeating him and the evil that he so powerfully spread.

5

If value consists in degrees of being, it follows that some sort of comparison of values is possible. But not everything that has a quantitative aspect is precisely measurable, and we need not expect to be any more successful than Jeremy Bentham if we look for a calculus of value. Where the degrees of actualization of a substance are related as AB to A, we are entitled to say without hesitation that AB is more valuable than A. But between A and B, between two possible forms of life, for example, that the same person might adopt, it is by no means easy to decide which better corresponds with his potentialities. What is of practical importance is to make an honest choice in accordance with the probabilities and to abide honestly by the choice made unless it turns out to be intolerable, but that is a matter of ethics rather than of metaphysics.

An even rougher comparison is possible between different things than is possible between different actualizations of the same thing. Whether philosophers are more important than poets, and either more important than plumbers, are scarcely questions which call urgently for an answer. The philosopher, the poet and the plumber can appropriately get on with their respective jobs without struggling for precedence. But a hierarchy of types of being is both a feature of traditional philosophy and susceptible of general justification. A living thing has a specific kind of activity which exceeds inorganic nature; to be sentient is more than to be merely alive; to think is more than to be merely sentient. Apart from these comparatively clear degrees of being comparison is not very rewarding. It is scarcely reasonable to ask whether it is better to be a rose than to be a tulip or better to be a dog than to be a cat.

It is still more hazardous to ask what would be the best kind of world. Is it one in which no type of thing is admitted which could be a source of harm to others, supposing that this is a possible kind of world at all, or one in which the variety of possible things is more completely displayed in spite of rivalry and conflict? Is it one in which there is free choice with all its momentous consequences of good and evil or one in which all tendencies are overruled for good? Human reason does not seem capable of making any answer. Still more, it seems that such worlds represent alternative and incompatible kinds of value. Hence the questions, what is the best possible kind of world and whether this is the best possible world, are probably nonsensical.

It is more to the point to ask how value is manifested by the various kinds of thing which make up the world we know. Inorganic nature does not show any obvious variation of value and disvalue. The inorganic thing is what it is and occupies its place in the order of being, whatever may be the relationships into which it enters. While its activity must be in accordance with its nature, its alternatives of realization seem to be alternatives of equal value. Hence teleological considerations are irrelevant to physics and chemistry.

Biology, however, .cannot dispense with teleological thinking. A plant, tree or vegetable is in a quite literal sense healthy or unhealthy and achieves a greater or a lesser development. Such differences in actualization or value are precisely what interests the biologist from both a theoretical and a practical point of view, and he would be foolish if he thought that his kind of science could eventually dispense with teleology. For an organism is a self-maintaining, self-developing and self-reproducing structure, and that is to be essentially a teleological unit.

An animal, a sentient organism, is also and evidently a teleological unit capable of more or less complete realization in accordance with its natural potentialities. A thinking mind, whether in association with an organism or not, is evidently capable of greater or lesser actualization or may be frustrated and deprived of its natural development. Here in the middle of the scale of being comes the full force of the alternatives of good and evil.

At the upper end of the scale absolute being is necessarily and timelessly all that being can be. Here is no alternative of intrinsic good or evil; the fullness of intrinsic value must belong without question to the fullness of being. Such a being, however, is beyond the world of ordinary human experience, and the question of its existence belongs not to general metaphysics but to natural or philosophical theology.

This whole doctrine of value as degree of being and fulfilment of nature commends itself as explaining why we use emotive language and why we experience desire and aversion. It does not deny that some ostensible value-judgments are merely expressions of emotion or that others merely state that we have this or that attitude of mind. It is only too clear that we often speak without thinking or without thinking sufficiently. But, when we do think, the test of the justification of our emotions or attitudes of mind is to be found in an objective criterion, and that criterion when analysed turns out to be the recognition that value consists in degree of being and fulfilment of nature while disvalue resides in frustration and privation of being,

CHAPTER X

Causality in Aristotle and Hume

I

THE DISCUSSION both of change in general and of substance as a unit of activity demands to be completed by a doctrine of causality, for causality in its most general sense signifies any way in which one state of fact emerges from another. Once again we may turn to Aristotle, whose causal theory dominated European philosophy for so many centuries. The fourfold division of causes is to be found in *Physics*, ii, 3, and is briefly repeated in *Metaphysics*, *Δ*, 2.

Aristotle recognizes no absolute beginnings, either of the world as a whole or of anything in it. The types of things are eternal although individual members of species come to be and perish, and in their ultimate substratum of reality things themselves are eternal although subject both to accidental and to substantial change. At least the things of this sublunary world are thought of as subject to substantial change; the heavenly bodies are incorruptible although eternally in a process of local movement.

Hence for Aristotle, every change in a positive direction involves a persistent substratum and a new character which this acquires. The substratum out of which and in which something comes to be is the material cause, and the novelty is the formal cause. This is of wider application than the distinction of first matter and substantial form by which Aristotle explains substantial change in the corporeal world. It applies also to accidental change, in which the substance as a whole is a material cause in relation to the new accidental form, and to change in incorporeal things, for a mind is a material cause in relation to the impressions which it receives. The agent which sets a change going or brings it to a stop is the efficient cause, and the end or purpose of the change is the final cause.

It is easy to see that this division of causes finds its fullest and most literal meaning in purposive human action. To take an eminently Aristotelian example, the sculptor, the efficient cause, takes a block of marble, the material cause, and fashions it into the shape of some god or hero, the formal cause. His purpose or final cause is to produce a great work of art or to earn his living or, more probably, both. That the Aristotelian division of causes should be derived in the first place from human activity need not surprise us if we remember that, prior to and apart from philosophy, the notion of causality has its primary significance in relation to human concerns and to the point at which human intervention can affect the process of events. As R. G. Collingwood pointed out, a cause in ordinary speech often means the motive on account of which someone does something, as when "we say that a solicitor's letter causes a man to pay a debt, or that bad weather causes him to return from an expedition".[1] In another common colloquial sense, "a cause is an event or state of things which it is in our power to produce or prevent, and by producing or preventing which we can produce or prevent that whose cause it is said to be".[2] Thus, turning the switch is said to be the cause of the light's coming on.

In his division of causes Aristotle may be said to have been halfway between the anthropomorphism of uncriticized common sense and a full measure of philosophical generalization. He was not himself unaware that his division was not as clear-cut as it might at first appear to be. If the sculptor's

[1] R. G. Collingwood, "On the so-called Idea of Causation", in *Proceedings of the Aristotelian Society*, 1937–8, p. 86.
[2] Collingwood, p. 89.

primary aim was to produce a work of art, then the statue itself was his end; the formal and the final causes coincided. In this case, moreover, the production of the work of art was a feature of his own development as a sculptor; the formal and final causes were also the actualization of the efficient cause. This becomes still more obvious if we think of what Aristotle took to be the chief end of man, the exercise of theoretical knowledge. Knowledge is not only the formal cause of an activity, but this activity is the immanent perfection of the efficient cause, which is also the material cause, and it is its own end or final cause.

Another kind of modification must be made when our attention is not engrossed by a personal agency or something resembling it. It is natural enough to speak of this as *the* efficient cause, but in every observed change many conditions concur to bring about the result. To single out one of these as *the* efficient cause is psychologically rather than logically motivated. On the commonsense level we tend to emphasize personal agency, as we have just remarked, or in other cases the last condition to be fulfilled makes most impression on us. Thus we say either that I turned on the light or that the turning of the switch, the last condition whose fulfilment was observable, was the cause of the light. A more objective view must acknowledge that, whether a personal agency be included or not, it is always a sum of conditions which is the adequate antecedent of the result. Among these conditions is the previous state of the subject of change, which Aristotle called the material cause.

When creative causality is taken into account, as it is by medieval Aristotelianism, it has to be recognized that the presence of a material cause is not necessary. In the matter of final causality a distinction must be made between conscious purpose and the wider teleology which is implicit in the Aristotelian doctrine of potency and act. Conscious purpose is an element in the efficient cause; finality in a wider sense implies that activity is an expression of the nature of the agent and takes place in accordance with general laws.

We can now formulate the causal problem in a more modern way, in the way in which it presented itself in the eighteenth century when Hume made his onslaught on the concept of cause. The explanation of change is thought to reside in an originative relationship of a set of antecedents, which we call the cause, to a consequent, which we call the effect, in accordance with general laws. This seemed to fit in both with common sense and with Newtonian physics, but Hume's critical scrutiny found plenty of ground for dissatisfaction.

2

Hume, as usual, looks for the impression or impressions from which the idea of causation is derived. These cannot be a specific class of qualities, for the causal relation is thought to belong to all kinds of things. Hence its origin must be sought among the other classes of relation. Here we "find in the first place, that whatever objects are consider'd as causes or effects, are *contiguous*; and that nothing can operate in a time or place, which is ever so little remov'd from those of its existence".[1] Contiguity in time, however, is later said to be alone essential, since non-spatial impressions and ideas, such as sounds, tastes and smells and also such as desires, can be terms in a causal relation.[2] Contiguity in space may be held necessary only in the case of spatial impressions, such as those of sight and touch.

Another relationship is the priority in time of the cause to the effect. In the same later passage, however, it is said of the taste and smell of a fruit that "whichever of them be the cause or effect, 'tis certain they are always coexistent". Coexistence might seem to contradict priority, but it should probably be interpreted as contiguity, so that, if the

[1] Hume, *Treatise of Human Nature*, ed. Selby-Bigge, bk. i, pt. iii, s. 2, p. 75.
[2] *Human Nature*, bk. i, pt. iv, s. 5, pp. 235–9.

impression of taste calls up the idea of smell, taste is the cause, and, if the impression of smell calls up the idea of taste, smell is the cause; in both cases there is contiguity in time, but the difference of order reverses the attributions of cause and of effect.

Hume, then, finds no difficulty in arriving at the recognition that a cause is immediately prior in time to its effect, but that is obviously not the whole meaning of the causal relation. We do not usually suppose that everything that immediately precedes an event is the cause if it. It is useless to add that the cause produces the effect, for that is merely to say that it is the cause. Nevertheless "there is a *necessary connexion* to be taken into consideration; and that relation is of much greater importance, than any of the other two above-mention'd".[1]

Inspection of instances, however, does not reveal to Hume wherein this necessary connection consists. Hence he turns to examine the principle of causality in the form in which he understands this principle. It is commonly held that whatever begins to exist must be caused. Is there anything in the notion of a beginning of existence which will serve to explain the necessary connection of cause and effect?

Hume makes an easy game of demolishing attempts to demonstrate the principle of causality. Hobbes had said that, apart from a cause, there was no reason why a thing should begin to exist when and where it does, but, since the whole question is whether any reason can be found for its existence at all, this line of thought begs the question. Clarke maintained that, if a thing had no cause, it would have produced itself, but again the question is whether it needs to be produced or caused at all. The same comment applies to Locke's argument that what is produced without a cause is produced by nothing. And, as Hume says, it is still more frivolous to assert the causal principle on the ground that every effect must have a cause, for the question is whether

[1] *Human Nature*, bk. i, pt. iii, s. 2, p. 77.

things are effects or not. This argument is like saying, "because every husband must have a wife, that therefore every man must be marry'd".[1]

We must allow that Hume is in the right in rejecting these ingenuous pieces of reasoning, but his positive argument that the causal principle cannot be upheld requires examination. This runs "that as all distinct ideas are separable from each other, and as the ideas of cause and effect are evidently distinct, 'twill be easy for us to conceive any object to be non-existent this moment, and existent the next, without conjoining to it the distinct idea of a cause or productive principle".[2] Consequently there can be no absurdity in saying that a thing begins to exist without a cause and no logical necessity in the causal principle. The assumption of this argument is evidently that all entailments are analytic, that a relationship of notions is never evident in the abstract unless one notion be a part of the analysis of the other. Here it is Hume who is begging the question or at least trying to get away with a mere assertion of what is itself by no means evident.

Hume, having failed to find any objective justification of causal relations, falls back on a psychological inquiry into how they come to be believed. He finds the answer in repeated experience of similar successions of events. When in experience an event of a type A has been frequently followed by an event of a type B, then, by the association of ideas, if another event of the type A occurs, we naturally look forward to and expect an event of the type B. There is no reason in the events themselves why we should do so; the explanation is wholly psychological, in terms of belief, for a belief is simply "a lively idea related to or associated with a present impression".[3] Hence a cause is "an object precedent and contiguous to another, and where all the

---

[1] *Human Nature*, bk. i, pt. iii, s. 3, p. 82.
[2] *Human Nature*, bk. i, pt. iii, s. 3, p. 79.
[3] *Human Nature*, bk. i, pt. iii, s. 7, p. 96.

objects resembling the former are plac'd in like relations of precedency and contiguity to those objects, that resemble the latter", or "an object precedent and contiguous to another, and so united with it, that the idea of the one determines the mind to form the idea of the other, and the impression of the one to form a more lively idea of the other".[1]

To call this an explanation of causal beliefs is, of course, nonsense, for the explanation is a causal law of, presumably, the same type as that which it seeks to explain. If it is an observed fact that events of a type A are frequently followed by events of a type B but no reason can be found why this should be so, it is equally an observed fact, that when two ideas have been frequently associated, the occurrence of the one is often followed by the expectation of the other but, on Hume's principles, no reason can be found why this should be so. Both processes being equally inexplicable, neither can serve as an explanation of the other. It remains from Hume's analysis that we do observe repeated successions of the same types of event, that afterwards we expect the one type of event to be followed by the other, but that no reason can be found for either of these empirical generalizations. These conclusions are far from satisfactory to the desire for understanding, and Hume himself is the first to admit their unsatisfactoriness, but he defies us to show how we can escape them in the realm of theory, even if we cannot accept them in the realm of practice.

3

"Hume without scepticism" is the title of a recent article on Hume's doctrine of causality, but the idea goes back almost to the time of Hume himself. The question is whether it is possible to adopt his analysis without implicitly denying ourselves to know what we really know that we know. Hume himself had no illusions. He agreed that, while he could not answer his own difficulties, no one could be content in

[1] *Human Nature*, bk. i, pt. iii, s. 14, p. 170.

practice to hold so negative a theory. We had only to turn
our minds from his arguments and our customary beliefs
would reassert themselves.

In a sense Kant is the first to put forward Hume without
scepticism, for he accepts from Hume that the causal
relation cannot simply be discovered in the material of
experience; it is an importation of the mind to make experience intelligible and is justified precisely because
experience would not be intelligible without it. Its validity,
therefore, belongs in the theoretical order entirely to the
realm of phenomena, to things as they appear. That
there must be something like it in the noumenal realm
seems to follow from what Kant says of the activity of the
transcendental Ego, but we cannot on Kant's principles
make this an object of theoretical knowledge. As ordinary
thinkers and as scientists, apart from moral activity, we must
be content with purely phenomenal causality. In this way
Hume is partly justified and partly transcended.

Others have tried on a more empirical basis to adapt
Hume's doctrine in such a way as to avoid an unplausible
degree of scepticism. The first of these seems to have been
Thomas Brown, the author of an *Inquiry into the Relation of
Cause and Effect* which dates from 1818. Hume admits both
that we observe similar sequences of antecedent and consequent and that in such cases we cannot help believing that
another instance of the antecedent will be followed by another
instance of the consequent. What more, asks Brown, do we
need in order to validate the causal relation? For, according
to him, the meaning of causation resides in uniformity of
sequence. A cause is "that which immediately precedes any
change, and which, existing at any time in similar circumstances, has been always, and will be always, immediately
followed by a similar change".[1] Nor could we have better
evidence for such uniformities of sequence than what he

[1] T. Brown, *Inquiry into the Relation of Cause and Effect*, 4th ed., London 1835,
p. 13.

variously describes as irresistible belief or instinct or intuition. If he meant intuition in the precise sense of direct insight, this would be a new, although highly disputable, assertion, but in fact he seems to use the term as equivalent to instinct or irresistible belief. The whole point of Hume's analysis, however, is to show that, although we observe repeated instances of similar sequences, no finite number of such observations can by themselves justify a universal affirmation, so that, as long as we bear Hume's analysis in mind, our instinctive causal beliefs cease to be irresistible. They regain their force, according to Hume, when we forget his reasoning, but Brown's attempt to assert their irresistibility in conjunction with Hume's analysis is an attempt to combine the incompatible.

Professor R. B. Braithwaite once defended the positive adequacy of a Humian analysis of causation on the ground not so much that our belief was irresistible as that there was no reason why we should resist it.[1] We have many beliefs for which we have forgotten the evidence, and we should be rash to claim an exhaustive knowledge of all the types of evidence which can justify a belief. Why, therefore, should we want to resist a belief in causal laws which seem to work in practice? The difficulty, however, still remains that Hume has analysed the grounds of our causal beliefs and that, if his analysis is correct, they are evidently inadequate.

R. E. Hobart manages to derive a positive theory from Hume by abandoning the demand that propositions should by either evident or demonstrable.[2] Appearances of fact are ultimate, and we ask proof for them only when faced with conflicting appearances. The principle of inductive generalization, however it is to be formulated, is an ultimate and unchallenged appearance of fact. Even if we

---

[1] "The Idea of Necessary Connexion", in *Mind*, Oct. 1927, pp. 467 sqq. and Jan. 1928, pp. 62 sqq.
[2] "Hume without Scepticism", in *Mind*, July & Oct. 1930, pp. 273 sqq., 409 sqq.

wanted to hold that no appearance was trustworthy without proof, this would itself be a generalization from experience and could not cast doubt on the principle by which we generalize from experience. Hence this principle is unassailable. Here we must say that the theory of knowledge involved is unacceptable. It is not true that everything that I can suppose to be possible is taken as fact unless there is contrary evidence. Nothing is an appearance of fact unless there is at least probable evidence for it, and, since probability is always dependent on evidence, the probable depends in the end on the evidently true. We are right, therefore, in looking for evidence for the inductive principle, and no positive theory can be built upon it in the absence of evidence.

In general we may add that there are cases when we do not know that a proposition is evidently or demonstrably true but we cannot help giving it a greater or lesser degree of assent. This implies that we believe ourselves to have had evidence for it at some time but that the evidence is no longer before our minds. It is contradictory, however, to say that we know a proposition to be neither evident nor demonstrable and yet that we cannot help believing it. As long as we remember that there is no evidence for it, we can and must help believing it. Hume was correct in thinking that his analysis led inevitably to scepticism about the causal relation.

4

The alternative, then, is either to embrace Hume together with scepticism or to supply and justify the element in the analysis of the causal relation which Hume omitted. This element is not far to seek, for the traditional view of causality evidently regarded the cause as making the effect intelligible. The cause was the explanation of the effect not only as providing another instance of a customary sequence but as showing reason for it. It was on account of the nature of the cause that the effect was of the kind it was, and sometimes at least we could directly understand why this sort of cause should have this sort of effect.

At much the same period as the two articles just cited, between twenty and thirty years ago, British philosophers began to consider whether the intelligible relation of cause and effect could not be restored in direct opposition to Hume. It was a time when Kantian and Hegelian idealism had lost its once large following and before the spread of logical positivism had renewed and enhanced the prestige of Hume. G. E. Moore had begun to speak of entailment propositions, by which he meant what Kant meant by *a priori* judgments, and, although he usually preferred analytic examples, the possibility of the *a priori* synthesis as a relation between types of fact no longer seemed to be excluded either by Hume's empiricism or by Kant's phenomenalism. Hence a number of thinkers began to ask whether causality could not be suitably analysed in terms of entailment. As an exceptionally clear example of this tendency of thought we will select for attention Dr. A. C. Ewing's "Defence of Causality."[1]

Ewing points out that, apart from the regularity of sequence which the disciples of Hume regard as the whole objective meaning of the causal relation, the ordinary man supposes, at least implicitly, that there is some intrinsic connection of dependence of the effect on the cause, that the cause helps to explain the effect and make it intelligible, that the cause is active in a sense in which the effect is not, and that the relation of cause and effect is necessary. All these points need elucidation and justification, but on the level of common sense they show that the regularity analysis of causality is not all that is held by the plain man.

He goes on to show that, if the regularity analysis is accepted as complete, it can only contradict what the plain man supposes. For it implies that there is no real dependence, no intrinsic intelligibility in the causal relation, no real

[1] In *Proceedings of the Aristotelian Society*, 1932–3, pp. 95–128.

activity, and no necessity in the connection of cause with effect. The regular sequence of this kind of antecedent with this kind of consequent becomes sheer coincidence and brute fact.

Moreover, even the disciple of Hume feels some need to justify his expectation that the future will resemble the past, unless he is content to sink into Hume's own complete theoretical scepticism. No theoretical justification can be found simply in an observed regularity in the past, nor will a pragmatic justification do, for this will extend only as far as the already observed facts which have succeeded the first tentative generalization. Any serious attempt to show or to make probable that the future will resemble the past requires a principle which is not purely empirical. If this is so, we need not be shy of admitting other non-empirical elements if necessary.

In order to do justice to our experience of causality we must admit that there is some real counterpart to the relationship of entailment. Entailment is primarily a logical relation between propositions, but one proposition could not entail another unless there were an equivalent relation between facts. To admit real entailment enables us to see that the effect is really dependent on the cause, that the cause explains the effect, and that the connection of cause and effect is necessary. The crux of the question, however, is whether we ever do apprehend such a relation between cause and effect. That we cannot do so in the events of the corporeal world is not an adequate objection, because we are insufficiently acquainted with its intrinsic nature; our knowledge of the corporeal world is external and relational.

Ewing thinks, however, that we have genuine insight into entailments in the psychological sphere or, if not of complete entailments, at least of intelligible causal tendencies. To become aware of a complete causal entailment would involve knowing all the relevant factors, but our partial knowledge is usually of factors which tend to operate but may be counteracted.

It seems to me that we can see and to some extent really understand why an insult should give rise to anger, why love should lead to grief if the object of one's love die or prove thoroughly unworthy, why a success should give pleasure. It does seem more reasonable on *other than inductive* grounds to suppose that if A loves B that will tend to make him sorry when B dies than to suppose that it will make him intensely glad, or that to be told he is a fool will be unpleasant rather than pleasant, when he thinks that the remark is really meant.[1]

Hence the deficiencies of a mere regularity analysis of causality and the need to introduce the element of entailment are borne out by experience. The precise meaning of what the plain man calls activity is not yet evident, but an entailment analysis of causality is justified both by abstract argument and by the facts of experience.

It is a pleasure to be able to refer to this clear and cogent paper as a sample of the reaction against Hume in the by no means distant past. More recently this kind of thinking has been swamped by the Humian revival which was called logical positivism. Nevertheless it still seems to indicate the path which we must tread if we are to exorcise the ghost of Hume. Our rightful discontent with an analysis which reduces the causal relation to an observed regularity of sequence leads us to ask further questions about it in terms of entailment and of the ontological relations which must be the foundation of logical entailments.

[1] "Defence of Causality", p. 124.

CHAPTER XI

Simultaneous and Successive Causation

I

WHILE entailment is in ordinary language equivalent to implication or the if-then relation, it is to be sharply distinguished from the special and arbitrary meanings given to implication in recent logic. It is said that a proposition p materially implies another proposition q when either p is false or q is true. This is no doubt part of the ordinary meaning of implication; if we say that "John is a man" implies that "John is mortal", we do mean at least that either John is not a man or John is mortal. But the terms of the definition are verified whenever both p and q are true; that is, any true proposition materially implies any other. They are also verified whenever p is false; that is, any false proposition materially implies any other proposition true or false. That this is not the ordinary meaning of implication is obvious.

A similar comment applies to what is called formal implication. This holds when, for all x, x is a materially implies that x is b. Again this is part of the meaning of implication, for, when we say that, if anything is coloured, it is extended, we do mean at least that it is not true in any instance both that this is coloured and this is not extended. But this logical relationship occurs whenever there are no instances of a. That x is a centaur formally implies that x likes plum jam, because, since there are no centaurs, there is no instance in which anything is a centaur and does not like plum jam. A logic in which a sentence such as "All centaurs like plum jam" has the same kind of validity as a sentence such as "All coloured things are extended" does not do justice to what we usually mean by an implication. We do not, of course, intend to derogate from the principle of Humpty Dumpty, by which anyone can define a term as he likes provided that he goes on to use it consistently with his definition, but we are concerned to rescue the ordinary meaning of implication from possible confusion.

The reason why material and formal implication as defined above are inadequate to ordinary thinking is evidently that they are defined exclusively in terms of logical extension, of what happens to be true. Entailment, or implication in the full sense of the word, is an intensional relation, a connection of meanings. It is a connection of propositions because it is primarily a connection of predicates or propositional functions. When we say that, if anything is coloured, it is extended, this is not because we have found this to be so in all instances but because we can perceive a connection between being coloured and being extended in two dimensions such that anything which is coloured must be extended in two dimensions. An entailment, therefore, is only another name for what is asserted in an *a priori* proposition or a genuine, as opposed to a merely enumerative, universal proposition. The question of entailment is at the root of the possibility of a deductive logic and of a fruitful metaphysic.

What sorts of relationship in fact enable us to assert entailment propositions? That there are analytic entailments is beyond dispute. It must always be true that, if anything is red, it is coloured, for being red is an instance of the range of characters summed up as being coloured. The real question is about the possibility of *a priori* synthesis. Here we would assert first of all that ontological presuppositions give rise to evident entailment propositions. We know that, if anything is coloured, it is extended, because we perceive that colour presupposes a two-dimensional expanse and we have no need to look for any other evidence than the clear connection of ideas. So also desire presupposes awareness; we can experience an obscure disquiet without any apparent object but desire is of an object present to the mind, and the emotion presupposes the presentation. The recognition of such instances of direct intellectual insight may, and indeed should, seem obvious enough to the philosophical novice, but it puts us at a stride beyond Hume's denial that completely distinct ideas could ever be necessarily related and, if we are convinced that awareness is of fact, it puts us also beyond Kant's phenomenalistic interpretation of the matter.

As far as causality is concerned, however, our business is not with ontological presuppositions but with what might by analogy be barbarously called ontological postsuppositions. Do we ever really perceive that one state of affairs must lead to another? Here we must observe that we do not only perceive complete entailments; we also, and much more frequently, perceive what Professor H. H. Price has called probabilifications, a useful word which deserves greater popularity than it has so far acquired.[1] That is to say, we are directly aware in many cases of the support which one proposition gives to another, even if it is not enough to establish it beyond doubt. The fact that an obituary notice appears in *The Times* makes it extremely probable that the person whose life it describes is dead; it does not entail his death, for it is possible and has actually happened that an obituary should be published by mistake. Much weaker probabilities are sufficient to induce people to risk their money on a race, but, apart from those innocents or cynics who select their horse by means of a pin, some sort of probability is required by those who put money on a horse. The obituary example was an example of a probable presupposition; the publication of an obituary probably presupposes, but does not absolutely presuppose, the death

[1] H. H. Price, *Truth and Corrigibility* (Inaugural Lecture, Oxford, 1936), pp. 9 sqq.

of the subject. A racing tip is an instance of a probable causal judgment; the known qualities of a particular horse, in comparison with the known qualities of the other horses competing, make probable that this horse will win the race although it is always erroneous to describe such a probability as a certainty.

Now there can really be no doubt that we are often directly aware, through a pure connection of meanings, of causal probabilifications in the logical order, which in the real order correspond with causal tendencies. Ewing's instances were mentioned in the previous chapter. It would be ridiculous to pretend that we expect success to give pleasure only because we have noticed it to do so in earlier instances; the connection is evident from the meanings of the terms. It would be ridiculous to wait for exhaustive inductive evidence before admitting that the awareness of danger tends to make a man devise and adopt measures to avoid it; the connection is immediately intelligible. Such connections are not infallible. Success has been known to have a bitter flavour when it comes too late; men, like rabbits, may be paralysed by fear in the face of danger. The connections are logically not entailments but probabilifications; ontologically they are not absolute causal laws but causal tendencies. But it is clear enough that we do discern parts of an intelligible pattern of change, especially in the order of events in our own minds, and that we expect greater knowledge to exhibit the pattern in greater detail. We have not yet arrived at the generalization that change arises from causal entailments which are the sum of the causal tendencies involved; such a generalization depends not on particular instances of insight but on the whole metaphysic of being. Nevertheless we can see that particular insights point towards such a generalization. Before making it, however, we have another difficulty to discuss.

2

In a paper on causality dating from 1912 Bertrand Russell tried to show that the relationship of causality to time was unintelligible and that, consequently, some different and more precise category was needed in order to interpret change. His argument is one to be taken seriously. It is generally supposed that the sequence of cause and effect is temporally immediate. But time does not consist of successive disparate moments; it is a continuum or, in Russell's terms, a compact series. Hence, if a cause is to be said to exist at all, it must exist for some finite time before the occurrence of the effect. But "it seems strange—too strange to be accepted, in spite of bare logical possibility—that the cause, after existing placidly for some time, should suddenly explode into the effect, when it might just as well have done so at any earlier time, or have gone on unchanged without producing its effect."[1] Moreover, if a cause can exist for a finite time without the effect, how can it be regarded as the complete cause of the effect and how can we avoid acknowledging that something might happen during this time to prevent the effect from taking place? "I put my penny in the slot, but before I can draw out my ticket there is an earthquake which upsets the machine and my calculations."[2]

R. G. Collingwood renewed this difficulty in 1938. We usually suppose that a cause is prior to its effect and that it determines its effect. But these two properties are incompatible. That which determines is necessarily simultaneous with that which is determined by it; what is prior cannot completely determine what is posterior. The guilt of attempting to combine these incompatible properties is attributed by Collingwood to Kant. For Kant had inherited

[1] B. Russell, "On the Notion of Cause", in *Mysticism and Logic*, London, 1932, pp. 184–5.
[2] "On the Notion of Cause", p. 187.

from Leibnitian rationalism the doctrine that cause and effect were related as ground and consequent; he accepted from Hume and from eighteenth-century science the view that cause preceded effect in time. "Their combination is therefore, to put it plainly, nonsense; a hybrid concept, deserving the description once given to the mule, as a creature having 'neither pride of ancestry nor hope of posterity'."[1] The Kantian mule has to be exposed and abandoned. That there are observed uniformities of succession is undeniable, but the attempt to interpret them as instances of determination of effect by cause is merely animistic; it is an unwarranted application of an in any case primitive mode of thinking about motivation and volition.

The surprising feature in Collingwood's account is the attribution of the usual view of causality to Kant. It appears really to be a great deal earlier than Kant. Whatever the language used, the notion that the causal relation explains temporal change by exhibiting a form of determination seems to belong to the whole Aristotelian tradition and to go back to Aristotle himself. Hence Collingwood is doing much more than merely attacking Kant, but the difficulty about time raised by Russell and himself is considerable.

If we take, as we have hitherto taken, the apparently natural view that the cause entails or determines the effect, both must be simultaneous. It might seem to follow that the world could have no history, for all causal determination would take place at once and history would be telescoped into a cosmic instant. Instead of explaining change we should thus have abolished it.

We might hasten to redress the position by insisting that a certain time-interval entered into the cause, so that the rest of the cause must always be separated from the effect by

---

[1] R. G. Collingwood, "On the so-called Idea of Causation", in *Proceedings of the Aristotelian Society*, 1937–8, p. 107.

that interval of time. We should thus have saved ourselves from the point of view of pure logic but not in any other way. For why should there be precisely this interval of time and not a longer or a shorter interval? More radically, how can the mere passage of time add anything to a cause? If we think we can see that cause entails effect, we can hardly deny that we can see equally clearly that the passage of time as such is irrelevant to the constitution of a cause. That is not the way out of the difficulty.

What Russell and Collingwood have really overlooked is the possibility of continuous change. They have tried to interpret causality in terms of successive instantaneous events, and it is no wonder that the flow of time thus forgotten should have taken its revenge upon them by appearing in the guise of an insurmountable difficulty. But the flow of time permits continuous change. Continuous change no doubt demands a cause, but a cause which is simultaneous with the effect. Discrete or instantaneous change becomes intelligible on a background of continuous change. When a continuous change has reached a certain limit, a discontinuity appears and a new event inaugurates a new beginning. Hegel's analysis of change is, therefore, to the point, for this is the celebrated transition in the dialectic from quantitative to qualitative change, and Hegel was right in thinking that qualitative presupposed quantitative change.

Indeed we may say that, apart from continuous change, history would be impossible. Hence, since there is history, since we experience the flow of time, continuous change must occur. We pointed out in a previous chapter that continuous change is not an object of direct experience, but we may now make amends by offering the reality of history as a premiss for a deductive proof of the occurrence of continuous change. If there were no continuous change, the whole history of the world would be telescoped into a moment.

Consequently, although change is to be explained in

causal terms, there is no principle that cause must be temporally prior to effect. An ontological priority is not necessarily a temporal priority. When we have recognized this, we have emancipated ourselves from the unduly restricted form in which the causal problem was considered by Hume and Kant, and we become able to avoid their mistakes and inadequacies. Moreover we can see that causal theory is not simply an explanation of change; dependence in being does not necessarily involve change or beginning. Even an instantaneous view of the world calls for explanation in terms of the causal interrelatedness of substantial natures or agencies. Everything is as it is on account of its relations with other things.

There is every reason, therefore, to distinguish a cause of being from a cause of becoming, *causa in esse* from *causa in fieri*. This distinction begins to emerge clearly in medieval philosophy. St. Thomas makes it explicitly, giving the builder and the cook as familiar examples of causes of becoming.[1] The builder is a cause of the house coming into existence, but, unless he is a very bad builder indeed, the house remains in existence, by virtue of the power of its materials to preserve their structure, for a considerable time after he has finished his work. The cook is a cause of food becoming cooked, but it remains cooked while changing in other respects after the cook has done with it. St. Thomas's example of a cause of being has lost its point on account of the overthrow of medieval physics, for it consists in an alleged continuous dependence of light on its source. It is easy enough, however, to devise another example such as the position of a book on a table; if the table collapses, the book does not remain suspended in the air but falls down also. Its position was continuously dependent on the presence of the table.

[1] *Summa Theologica*, I, q. 194, a. i.

3

Having thus enlarged our view of causality from the determination of temporal consequent by temporal antecedent upon which the gaze of Hume and Kant was concentrated, and having taken account both of continuous change and of causation in being, we may usefully attempt to sketch a synthesis of what we mean by cause and effect. We need to discriminate simultaneous causation in being, simultaneous causation in becoming and successive causation in becoming.

Change does not enter into the conception of *simultaneous causation in being.* The world consists of substances upon whose interrelation depend the actual qualities and activities which they manifest at any given moment. The field of interrelation in the world of experience is space, taken not as an independent container of objects but as a field set up by the actual relations of bodies as extended in three dimensions. The nature of a thing manifests itself and is active in what it actually is. That is why we speak of many of its manifestations as its activities and could reasonably extend the meaning of the term to all its manifestations. It is natural to say that I am active in thinking and speaking, in walking and running, in eating and drinking; it would be significant to speak of myself as active in more fundamental qualities such as volume and shape, for these are being actively maintained. Aristotle's conception of actuality does in fact cover all attributes and not only what it is usual in English to call activities.

Such is *immanent* simultaneous causation in being. In Aristotelian terms I, as a nature with a teleology or final cause, am the efficient cause of the qualities and activities to which my substance is again related as material to formal cause. But I am not the whole cause of my qualities and activities; what these are at any moment is largely dependent on circumstances, that is, upon the other things with which I am in spatial relation. Their causal relation to what I am at the moment is *transeunt* simultaneous causation in being.

I am aware of simultaneous causation in being in my contact with other bodies. For contact is not merely contiguity of volume but mutual pressure of mass. My fundamental awareness of myself as embodied is of myself as a corporeal mass in active contact with other corporeal masses. Hence Whitehead was right in saying that "the perception of conformation to realities in the environment is the primitive element in our external experience."[1]

Simultaneous causation in becoming is the relation of determining conditions to continuous change. Once again these conditions include the nature of the changing thing as well as the external circumstances which stimulate the change. Since the occurrence of continuous change is a matter of inference, it is not easy to give an unassailable example, but we tend reasonably to suppose that certain stretches of local movement are continuous and that things do not jump from one place to another without traversing the intervening space. Hence the internal and external conditions which determine an object to move from one place to another will do as a generally accepted example.

Continuous change, however, has its limits. Water gradually becomes hotter and then suddenly becomes steam; it gradually becomes colder and then suddenly becomes ice. That will serve as a pattern of events in every sphere of being. In the psychological sphere, for instance, I gradually become more annoyed while retaining my patience and then suddenly lose my patience and say all that I think or rather more. Two nations gradually become more estranged while remaining at peace until some possibly small but decisive event occurs and war breaks out. The proverb about the last straw enforces the notion of transition from quantitative to qualitative change.

[1] A. N. Whitehead, *Symbolism*, Cambridge, 1928, p. 51.

Here, then, we have the situation to which *successive causation in becoming* is relevant and in which we look for a determining connection between antecedents and consequents. Instances of partial direct insight into such connections are common in the psychological sphere. We can see more or less why our thoughts took a certain course, why we were pleased or annoyed, why we felt attracted by one thing and repelled by another. While the psychologists are justified in warning us not to suppose that a superficial glance tells us all we might know about the sources of our thoughts and desires, it would be ridiculous to go to the other extreme and to hold that no connections of this kind were ever obviously valid.

We must say again that it was unfortunate that the attention of Hume and Kant was exclusively devoted to successive causation in becoming, and that in the corporeal world, where direct insight is almost lacking and we have to fall back on observed uniformities of sequence as probable evidence of causal laws. Being, like everyone else, unable to see how one billiard ball communicates movement to another and observing only that billiard balls happen to behave in a more or less uniform way, Hume rashly concluded that uniformity of sequence was the sole objective element in causal laws. His narrowness of view has been enthusiastically copied by empirical philosophers ever since, with the regrettable result that causality is regarded as a gratuitous importation by some primitive metaphysician instead of a very obvious fact of experience.

The wider view that we have taken of causation also takes the sting out of the suggestion that the causal problem is not of importance because the more developed sciences are not interested in causal laws. It may well be true that causal sequences are now of less moment to science than they were in the Newtonian atmosphere breathed by Hume and Kant, but on a more adequate view of causation all correlations must depend on causal connection of one kind or another. If there were no such connections, there would be no hope of even approximating to constant correlations. The scientist, faced with well-established uniformities, could only suppose himself to be the victim of a degree of coincidence which would amount to a cosmic hoax. It is scarcely in the scientific spirit to maintain a philosophy which denies the presuppositions of scientific inquiry; the scientist, if he is to be a philosopher at all, should recognize that his pursuits presuppose a metaphysic. Apart from metaphysical principles a scientist would not know even to be probable and approximate what he does know at least to be probable and approximate.

A few words might be added to connect the philosophical theory of causation with the colloquial use of causal terms. The full causal conditions of any thing or event, of any instance of being or of becoming, are complex and various. Colloquially, however, we tend to speak of *the* cause of an event. The selection of the condition which we describe as *the* cause is clearly pragmatic and depends upon the object of our main interest. Naturally we think of persons as causes in a special sense, since they are capable of partially foreseeing and intending the results of their actions. When the householder asks the boys who broke the window, he is not likely to be mollified by an accurate description of the conditions under which missiles are able to penetrate glass; he wants to know the human agency at work. When we ask for *the* cause of something, we are often inquiring into the purposive human activity involved and are indifferent to the other necessary conditions.

In other cases it is the last differential condition to be fulfilled that engages our attention. If we see water coming through the ceiling, we do not ask for a disquisition on the sources of the local water supply but want to know where the break has occurred which occasions the deluge. That, for us, is *the* cause of the water coming through the ceiling. There can, therefore, be many sorts of pragmatic justification for speaking of *the* cause of an event although we really know that a multiplicity of causal conditions have to be fulfilled. When we are trying to think with full objectivity, however, we have to consider the whole sum of causal conditions, everything, that is, on which the existence of a thing or the occurrence of an event depends. In doing so we need to distinguish simultaneous causation of being, simultaneous causation of continuous change and successive causation of discrete change, and our view of the world as a causal system is incomplete unless all these types of connection are given their due. They are all, however, types of entailment of the ontologically posterior by the ontologically prior, for that is what is meant by causality in general.

CHAPTER XII

Principles of Causality and Intelligibility

I

MUCH TIME has been devoted to the discussion of the principle of causality. It might be wiser to speak of principles of causality, for different philosophers have proposed different formulae with different meanings, but, whether we use the singular or the plural, we have to ask if there are any valid general maxims which may help to guide our search for causes in practice. First of all, however, we must glance at the principles of contradiction and identity, for these are of even greater generality and are sometimes supposed to give rise to the principle of causality.

The principle of contradiction, as formulated by Aristotle, states that the same attribute cannot at the same time belong and not belong to the same subject in the same respect.[1] Evidently the qualifications of *the same time* and *the same respect* are intended to sharpen the sameness of the attribute, so that the principle could be more sparely stated in the form that a thing cannot be both A and not-A. That means that, if a thing is A, it is not not-A, or if a thing is A, it is other than what is other than A.

The principle of identity might be traced back to the saying of Parmenides that *being is*, but this really has a fuller and more concrete meaning and is intended to assert that being simply is and does not come to be or cease to be or change. The notion that an abstract principle of identity is presupposed by the principle of contradiction and is the

[1] Aristotle, *Metaphysics*, Γ, 3, 1005 b, 19.

163

absolutely first principle seems to be a product of later medieval logic and is sometimes attributed to the Scotist Antonius Andreas (d. about 1320). What, then, does it mean to say that everything is what it is? As it stands, the sentence is obviously tautological. If we ask what is meant to be conveyed by it, the answer might be that everything is identical with itself. But identical means *not other*, and not other means *other than other*. In this case, therefore, the principle of identity, like the principle of contradiction, would mean that everything is other than what is other than itself.

It does not seem, then, that in the end the principles of identity and contradiction state anything except the symmetrical character of the relation of *otherness*, and of the two the principle of contradiction states it more clearly and directly. If *otherness* were not a symmetrical relation, of course, affirmation and negation would be meaningless, and it is on this account that the principle of contradiction deserves to be called the first principle, or perhaps better the first presupposition, of rational discourse. It is not only true but absolutely undeniable, for the denial of it makes denial meaningless; if any philosopher is said to deny it, this can only be in a sense different from that in which it is asserted. Hegel and Bergson, for example, would in their different ways judge the principle of contradiction to be inadequate to a reality which they allege to be in constant flux and so never unambiguously to be anything. Our quarrel with such philosophers is not about the principle of contradiction but about the primacy of being over becoming. In general, the principle of contradiction is essential to intellectual life, as the air that we breathe is essential to physical life, but, also like the air that we breathe, it can usually be taken for granted.

Still less can even the most prolonged contemplation of the principles of identity and contradiction give rise to a principle of causality, for causality is a notion not contained in them, and it is quite impossible to draw out of any philosophical hat notions which are not there. Whatever is true about causality must have its own evidence and cannot be reduced to principles into which causality does not enter. Those who have sought the origin of the principle of causality in the principles of identity and contradiction have presumably been misled by a misapplication of the truth that a caused thing would not be what it is without a cause. But the point of this is not that it would thus be other than what it is, so overthrowing the principle of contradiction, but that it would not be at all. The connection between effect and cause remains synthetic in the Kantian sense and cannot be generated from a mere contemplation of the being of the effect. We need specific experience of instances of cause and effect before we can begin to generalize about causality. Hence we must consider the principle of causality in its own terms and with its own evidence.

2

In formulating a principle of causality it is not easy to avoid the extremes of either uttering a tautology or going beyond what is really evident. An obvious example of a tautology would be the statement that every effect has a cause, for an effect means what is caused and a cause means what has an effect. There may, however, be less obvious tautologies, and one is the statement that everything contingent has a cause. This is sometimes actually put forward as the proper form of the principle of causality.

But what is meant by contingency? The contingent is often defined as what exists but *might not exist*. This is inaccurate, for, if it exists, there is no possibility that it might not exist. What is meant is rather that it *might not have existed*. The contingent is rightly described as that which exists but might not have existed. But, once more, what is meant by saying that it might not have existed? We might be disposed to answer that there is no contradiction in supposing it not to exist, but this is scarcely satisfactory, for it would mean that nothing entails that it exists, and, if it does exist, something, which is its cause, evidently does entail that it exists. If we said that there is no *intrinsic* contradiction in supposing it not to exist, this would mean either that it does not itself entail that it exists or that there is no general character of fact which entails that it exists. It is difficult to put any precise meaning on either of these sentences. A thing cannot literally entail its own existence, for it would have to exist before it existed. In the latter case, while it is not absurd when talking of the impossible to say that a general character of fact entails its non-existence, it is scarcely plausible to make a general character of fact a possible source of real existence.

There seems to be no doubt in the end that, when we express ourselves appropriately, what we mean by saying that the contingent *might not have existed* is that it *would not have existed* without a cause. Hence the distinction between necessary and contingent being coincides not only in fact but also in meaning with the distinction between uncaused and caused being. To say that everything contingent is caused is, therefore, true but tautologous. If we want to assert a significant principle of causality, we must look for some indication of being caused which is not synonymous with it.

The most commonly accepted indication of being caused is a beginning of existence. Hence the principle of causality has most usually been formulated as a statement that what begins to exist is caused or that every change demands a cause. In this form the principle may be said to have been a commonplace of practically the whole of European philosophy before Hume. Thus Plato declares that every thing that comes to be must come to be through some cause, for it is impossible to have a beginning without a cause.[1]

[1] Plato, *Timaeus*, 28, A.

Aristotle's fourfold doctrine of cause is an elaboration of the conditions which make becoming intelligible. An odd dissentient voice like that of Nicholas of Autrecourt, who in the fourteenth century denied the necessity of the principle of causality on grounds similar to Hume's, only emphasizes its general acceptance in medieval philosophy.

The case is not the same with Aristotle's principle that everything moved is moved by something other than itself. For Aristotle did really think that a corporeal thing could not be the source of its own motion and that only mind could be a self-moved mover. This is in obvious conflict with Newton's first law of motion, that every body perseveres in uniform motion in a straight line except when it is affected by impressed forces. The difference here is really one of physical hypothesis, although Aristotle seems to have persuaded himself that he could establish his point by an absolute philosophical argument and Newton may have had equal confidence in the necessity of his own law. For, philosophically, it is equally possible to think of a body as moved by another and to think of it as being in an intrinsic condition of motion, and the only grounds for preferring one view to the other must come from the way in which it fits in with the facts of observation. A certain ambiguity shows itself in the application of the notion of change. Is any motion to be regarded as a change or is it only a change in a state of motion which is a genuine change?

It becomes clear that, while it may well be evident in some sense that what begins to exist must be caused, we have first to determine the sense in which we are using our terms. After all, a cause may be a cause of becoming or a cause of being; it may be temporally antecedent or temporally simultaneous. Since a cause is a sum of conditions, causation may be partial or complete; it may be an incomplete stimulus or an absolute determination of the effect.

Hence Kant's principle, even if transferred from the sphere of phenomena to things in themselves, is too narrow. For

Kant thought that it was a maxim of scientific investigation to presuppose and to seek the determining antecedents of any event. But there is always room for the intervention of a creative causality, which is timeless. Moreover, in the case of a free choice, we think of the antecedents as motivating but not as determining; the event is not antecedently determined but is in a special way the present act of the agent. Any satisfactory principle of causality must make allowance for at least these two points.

The easiest way to approach what is really self-evident is by considering what it would mean to be totally uncaused. Consider a being which has neither complete nor partial cause of its becoming or of its being. Such a being, I would venture to say, is self-evidently timeless and changeless, without a beginning or an end of its existence. Since the totally uncaused has no beginning of existence, it follows by conversion that what begins to exist is not totally uncaused. Let us take this as a first approximation to acceptable principles of causality and explore its consequences.

What comes to be must certainly have an adequate cause of being, for what has no cause of being must simply exist timelessly and changelessly and, since it has no becoming, has no cause of becoming. But we cannot say that what comes to be must necessarily have temporal antecedents, for the cause of its being may also be the cause of its becoming either wholly or partially. A creative causality is the timeless cause both of the becoming and of the being of what is created. In a free choice the simultaneous causality of the agent supplies what is lacking in the temporal antecedents of the act, which are motivating but not determining. Hence we may conclude that what begins to be has an adequate cause of being and may have temporal causal antecedents. The final phrase can be strengthened by the consideration that even a free act has partial causal antecedents in the shape of motives and that in an ordered world it is not to be expected that creative causality should be constantly intervening.

Such is the way in which coming-to-be is an indication of being caused, but it does not appear to be the only possible indication. Since causality in general implies ontological but not necessarily temporal priority, we can conceive of something as being caused without having begun to exist but existing in an eternal causal dependence. The fact that we know of no such thing will not deter the metaphysician from examining the theoretical case. If, then, we remove the thought of a beginning in time, what is the fundamental indication of the need of a cause? The final answer must lie in finitude. Only that being can be uncaused which is altogether being and without limitation all that being can be. Whatever is finite and limited must be caused. Wherever there is the metaphysical composition of being and quiddity, a cause of being is demanded. These conclusions, of course, bring us to philosophical theology, but we are indeed compelled to recognize that our causal principles are not completely formulated until we are at the threshold of philosophical theology.

3

Reverting to general metaphysics and its logical applications, we can now see the ontological background of inductive generalization. Where, as in the sphere of mind, we have a certain measure of insight into causal tendencies, we have only to refine upon our initial insights by more exact thinking and more detailed observation, but such insight seems to be lacking in respect of the material world. Our generalizations about the behaviour of material things, whether on the level of common sense or on the level of science, arise from observation of actual uniformities. What justification do such observed uniformities give to our generalizations?

The history of inductive logic shows a recurrent dilemma. On the one hand, the scientist and the logician of scientific method may be impatient of metaphysics and may seek the whole foundation of the validity of inductive inference in observation. In this case Hume made very clear, and all rational persons have since admitted, that no finite number of observed uniformities can by themselves lend even a probability to a genuine universal proposition. For a genuine universal proposition covers not only all actual cases, most of which, whether in past, present or future, are outside our observation, but also all possible cases, which make up an innumerable multitude. No finite number bears any proportion to infinity. No finite number of instances, therefore, can be evidence for a generalization. It does not matter how many times you have seen hydrogen and oxygen in due proportion combining into water; there are an infinite number of actual and possible cases which you have never observed and in which, as far as observation goes, they might do nothing of the kind.

Nor is it enough to say that, while a theoretical justification of inductive methods is lacking, theoretical justification does not matter; pragmatic justification suffices. For a pragmatic justification can lie only in the fact that scientific laws have hitherto worked with a sufficient degree of accuracy; it can give us no shadow of guarantee about the future. The future as such is an empirical matter for none of us. If we left the question there, an unbridgeable gulf would remain between our logical thinking and our psychological expectations. That is, of course, precisely what Hume asserted to be so, but we may by this time agree that the value of Hume resides in his being a tough obstacle to overcome rather than a master to follow. Common sense tells us that we really know rather more than Hume would allow us to know, but common sense by itself cannot tell us what precisely this is and how we know it.

On the other hand, many logicians have tried to supply inductive methods with a theoretical justification by appealing to a principle of the uniformity of nature. The difficulty in the absence of an adequate metaphysic has been to say what exactly this principle is and on what grounds it can be asserted. Another difficulty arises from this apparently being a causal principle and, if the causal relation be understood, as it generally has been in modern times, in the narrow sense of a determining relation of temporal antecedents to a temporal consequent, from the more radical doubt whether the sciences, and especially physics, are much concerned with causal laws in this sense. Perhaps the philosophers in their kindness of heart and their ignorance of science are trying to offer to the scientists a theoretical basis for something which the scientists themselves are not in the least concerned to do. This is a criticism which should be fairly familiar to readers of Bertrand Russell. Such, then, is the dilemma of inductive logic. Apart from metaphysical principles it seems to be without a theoretical basis, but an equal difficulty appears when we try to find the appropriate metaphysical principle and to ask why it should be asserted.

Approaching the question in another way, there is no difficulty in appreciating the negative value of observation in relation to possible generalizations. One instance of a thing of the type A not followed or accompanied by a thing of the type B is sufficient to disprove the generalization that every A must be followed or accompanied by a B. If there is some initial positive probability, however small, it is intelligible that the possible generalizations which survive the test of a systematic investigation of negative instances should gradually increase their probability to an imposing extent. The difficulty lies in assigning and rationally justifying the initial probability.

The task of the appropriate metaphysical foundation of inductive logic is not to provide an unassailable major premiss with the aid of which induction can be converted into deduction but to lend some initial probability to the first tentative generalizations which emerge from our ordinary experience. No absolute principle of the uniformity of nature appears to be available, but metaphysics can show us that the world consists of substances acting in accordance with

171

their natures and that the actual state of the world is a consequence of causal correlations both simultaneous and successive. The exceptions to absolute regularity resulting from the activity of personal wills are not such as to overrule the general picture of regularity. Hence it is worth while to look for regular correlations in the world, and those uniformities which persist in different circumstances enjoy some measure of probability in approximating to such natural correlations.

Thus, on the level of common sense, we recognize the similarity of certain states of affairs which we call instances of fire and notice that many things when brought into contact with them will burn. We do not know precisely what fire is or precisely what burning is, nor are we in the least entitled to be unprepared for exceptions, but we can generalize to the extent of saying that fire usually burns. The logical status of commonsense generalizations is well expressed in the simple rules mentioned by Alice; "such as, that a red-hot poker will burn you if you hold it too long; and that if you cut your finger *very* deeply with a knife, it usually bleeds; and she had never forgotten that, if you drink much from a bottle marked 'poison' it is most certain to disagree with you sooner or later".

If an exception occurs to a commonsense generalization, our reaction may linguistically take more than one form. We may say "That is a queer fire—it does not burn"; or "That does not burn—it cannot be a fire." The real problem, however, remains in each case the same; it is to discover the significant difference among the things which we have hitherto regarded as instances of fire, whether we continue to call them all fire or not, which can be correlated with the difference between burning and not burning. In such wise, presumably, scientific investigation is born. The more irrelevancies are excluded and the more significant differences are taken into account, the greater the probability that surviving generalizations will approximate to true

172

general laws, although, since we cannot lay claim to an exhaustive knowledge of any situation, we can never be certain that we have excluded all irrelevancies and taken all significant differences into account. Hence inductive generalizations remain in the sphere of probability and approximation, although, granted an initial probability, their final probability may become very high.

When, therefore, the philosopher removes what is anthropomorphic in the commonsense idea of causality and frees its theoretical conception from the eighteenth-century restriction to temporal sequences, the general notion of causality comes near enough to the scientific concept of correlation. The scientist can well be asked to consider what sort of real relation must be the source of the correlations which he discovers or supposes to exist, and to admit that they can only be what the philosopher calls causal connections in a sufficiently wide sense of the phrase. It is because metaphysics reveals the world as a field of causal connections, simultaneous or successive, in being or in becoming, that the scientist's quest for observable uniformities is rationally justified.

4

Just as the principle of identity was an attempt to find something more fundamental than the principle of contradiction, so Leibniz proposed to go behind the principle of causality and to set up as a more general maxim the principle of sufficient reason. This is a principle "in virtue of which we hold that no fact can be genuine or existent and no proposition true unless there is a sufficient reason why it should be so and not otherwise, although, for the most part, these reasons cannot be known by us".[1] In other words, every thing and every true proposition either explains itself or demands an explanation beyond itself.

[1] Leibniz, *Monadology*, § 32.

As far as reality is concerned, what demands explanation is to be explained in causal terms, and the principle of sufficient reason does not yet seem to say anything different from the principle of causality in the tautological form that everything contingent is caused. Just as we still needed an indication by which to recognize the contingent, so Leibniz's principle leaves us needing an indication of what demands explanation beyond itself. We are still merely saying that what is caused is caused.

Leibniz's principle, however, is intended to apply also to the uncaused as what explains itself. But what is meant by a thing being the sufficient reason of its own existence? If this were to have any positive meaning, it would signify that a thing could be the source of its own existence, which is absurd, or that the essence of a thing could entail its existence, which is equally absurd, for the essence would then have to exist in at least logical priority to its existence. This is, of course, the ancient and familiar fallacy of the ontological argument. Hence, in the case of uncaused being, the principle of sufficient reason can only have a negative meaning; it must signify that the thing requires no explanation. So the principle can be reduced to a statement that a thing either needs no explanation or needs a causal explanation, which is the same as saying that a thing is either uncaused or caused. This truism was hardly worth Leibniz's trouble.

On the logical side the principle may likewise be reduced to the statement that every true proposition is either demonstrable or self-evident, but this, although it turns out to be no discovery of Leibniz but a characteristic doctrine of Aristotle and of the philosophical tradition, is not without significance. The principle of sufficient reason is, therefore, of logical rather than of metaphysical importance in the first place, but it has a metaphysical repercussion in so far as it implicitly anchors knowledge in the awareness of being. For it is only if we have a genuine awareness of being, and if

174

knowledge begins with a direct awareness of being, that there can be self-evident propositions. If knowing were always at a remove from being and its relationship to being were always problematic, we should have no criterion of truth but the coherence which serves in fact as a criterion of truth for the idealist. We can usefully say that truth consists in conformity with fact only if that conformity is not always a question for reflective comparison. If we had always to compare an idea with the fact which it purported to represent, we could really compare it only with another idea at an equal remove from the fact, for it would be implied that we had no direct knowledge of fact. It is because in the beginnings of knowledge there is a real unity of awareness and fact that we both have a genuine knowledge of fact and a direct awareness of the conformity of this knowledge with fact.

On this account the scholastics named truth as a transcendental property of being. *Omne ens est verum.* Truth in its primary meaning belongs to propositions as in conformity with fact, but being itself is said to possess truth in so far as it is the source and final guarantee of true knowledge. As knowledge is of being, so all being is in principle able to be known. That is very far from saying that we are able to know everything, but the limitations of our knowledge arise from the character of our minds and not from the nature of being itself. The principle of sufficient reason can, consequently, be given a real significance if it is interpreted as meaning that everything that exists is intelligible either through its own evidence or in virtue of something more fundamentally intelligible. Our own cognitive powers are limited but need never, apart from our own positive fault or negligence, be perverted, because they are of their nature directed to real being.

Moreover, as we saw when we dealt with the analytic and abstractive function of thinking, reality seems to reach its full stature only through being thought. If there are distinctions and relations in the logical order, to which no real distinctions and relations correspond, although fact is such as to enable these distinctions and relations to be asserted with logical validity, it would appear that being is of its nature destined to thought. This is the insight which is exaggerated in the idealist contention that there is no being save mind and its contents. While, in opposition to idealism, the distinct reality of the material world must be upheld as a primary evidence, the subordination of object to thought can scarcely be denied. The basic mode of reality must be mental rather than material.

In general, then, although the principles of sufficient reason, of contradiction and of causality need more critical analysis than they sometimes receive, their genuine significance survives criticism and appears clearly when vagueness and ambiguity are overcome. Of the traditional metaphysics of the Aristotelian school it is possible to say the same as a whole. They survive the criticism of Hume and cf Kant and of their respective followers, but the more closely that criticism is studied and the more honestly it is taken into account, the more clearly do the truths of metaphysics stand out. We need not fear that the work of metaphysics has to be begun again, but it is equally true that it has to be reviewed and renewed in every age in relation to the difficulties and problems of the age. Only if men neglect this need of constant and patient critical rethinking will metaphysics perish.